D0776948

Presented to:

_____

From:

_____

Date:

_____

The Treasure
of God's Word

Celebrating
400 Years
of the
King James Bible

Compiled by Jack Countryman

THOMAS NELSON

Since 1798

NASHVILLE   DALLAS   MEXICO CITY   RIO DE JANEIRO

The Treasure of God's Word

© 2010 by Jack Countryman

All rights reserved. No portion of this book may be reproduced, stored in a retrieval system, or transmitted in any form or by any means—electronic, mechanical, photocopy, recording, scanning, or other—except for brief quotations in critical reviews or articles, without the prior written permission of the publisher.

Published in Nashville, Tennessee, by Thomas Nelson®. Thomas Nelson is a registered trademark of Thomas Nelson, Inc.

Thomas Nelson, Inc., titles may be purchased in bulk for educational, business, fund-raising, or sales promotional use. For information, please email SpecialMarkets@ThomasNelson.com.

Scripture quotations are taken from the KING JAMES VERSION.

Articles adapted from *KJV 400—Celebrating the Legacy of the Bible,* © 2010 by Thomas Nelson, Inc.

Articles on pages 20 and 56 adapted from www.wikipedia.com.

ISBN-13: 978-1-4041-8976-8

Printed in China
10 11 12 13 14 15 — TIMS — 6 5 4 3 2 1

Contents

Introduction

On July 22, 1604, shortly after James VI of Scotland ascended the throne of England as King James I (1603), he announced a decision that history has shown was the watershed event of his reign: a new translation of the Bible was to be undertaken. The English translation of the Bible that appeared in 1611, the Authorized Version, known popularly as the King James Version, came to be regarded as the most influential book in the history of English civilization. Writers and literary critics have acclaimed it as the "noblest monument of English prose." In a series of lectures at Cambridge University during World War I, Sir Arthur Quiller-Couch declared the King James Version was "the very greatest" literary achievement in the English language.

Indeed, the King James Version is a living landmark in the history of the English language, both a religious and literary classic, and its influence has been incalculable. Adam Nicolson, author of *God's Secretaries*, writes that it "can lay claim to be the greatest work in prose ever written in English." Scholars have long agreed that the greatest influences in the shaping of the English language are the King James Version and the complete works of William Shakespeare. Throughout the history of the English language, the King James Version has remained the most often quoted document in existence—a constant inspiration to people from all walks of life, whether poets, farmers, pastors, housewives, or politicians.

This treasure of King James Scripture brings to light God's purpose and desire to share with us His great love, grace, and mercy with everyone who reads this book. We have chosen forty-five distinct passages illuminating God's everlasting love and compassion for those who choose to follow Jesus Christ. These passages are followed by additional Scriptures to shed further light on the vastness of God's love for each of us. We have also given the reader a pathway to understand our heritage and responsibility as Christians and followers. We are hopeful that these topical passages of Scripture will be a blessing to you, the reader, and draw you into a closer walk with our blessed Savior.

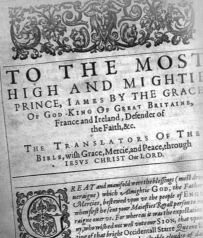

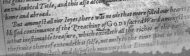

King James I, artist unknown
(Scottish National Portrait Gallery)

The Origins of the King James Bible

Even before King James took the throne in London, he was approached by a group of Puritans with a petition signed by 800 clergy that requested reform within the Church of England. The petition prompted the king to call for a conference of Anglican bishops, clergymen, and professors, along with four Puritan leaders, in January 1604 at Hampton Court "for the hearing, and for the determining, things pretended to be amiss in the church." Although a new translation of the Bible in English was not on the agenda, Dr. John Reynolds, the Puritan president of Corpus Christi College, Oxford, presented a strong case for the need of one. At the time, the Bishops' Bible was the standard in churches, but the Geneva Bible was the most popular English translation in homes.

King James, as well as others in England at the time, was not in favor of the Geneva Bible, because some of the Calvinist commentary in its marginal notes was felt to promote resistance to the king and state. He declared, "I could never yet see a Bible well translated in English; but I think that, of all, that of Geneva is the worst. I wish some special pains were taken for an uniform translation, which should be done by the best learned men in both Universities, then reviewed by the Bishops, presented to the Privy Council, lastly ratified by the Royal authority, to be read in the whole Church, and none other."

The Anglican bishop of London, Richard Bancroft, was not in favor of a new translation, but consented that if a new translation was to be undertaken, marginal notes must be kept to a minimum. Accordingly, a resolution came forth: "That a translation be made of the whole Bible, as consonant as can be to the original Hebrew and Greek; and this to be set out and printed, without any marginal notes, and only to be used in all churches of England in time of divine service." It was to be a Bible for everyone, and Bancroft would become its "chief overseer" as well as Archbishop of Canterbury.

The Cultural Background of the Translators

The historical stage was set for a translation of the Bible that would become the most cherished Bible translation of all time. Considered the golden age of English literature, the Elizabethan age of the late sixteenth century had brought a flowering of drama and poetry with writers such as Spenser, Marlowe, and Shakespeare. The most important dramas in English and a great deal of lyric poetry were produced during this period. Regarding the English language of the period, Adam Nicolson states: "Boisterous, elegant, subtle, majestic, finely nuanced, sonorous and musical, the English of that period has a more encompassing idea of its own reach and scope than any before or since. It is a form of the language that drips with potency and sensitivity." It was from within the context of this Renaissance of literature and language that the men who were appointed to translate the Bible from 1604 to 1611 were drawn—contemporaries of some of the greatest English authors of all time. The King James Version thus came to partake of the rhythms and the beauty of Elizabethan poetry and drama, perhaps the finest English has ever known.

Second, the translators were benefiting from the relatively new technology of the printing press, in much the way that today's world has been changed by the Internet. With the invention of printing in Germany by Johannes Gutenberg (c. 1450), the promoters of the new learning found a new technology at their disposal as well as the means to light the spark of the Protestant Reformation. Among the first products of the printing press were editions of the Bible—the very first major work being the famous Gutenberg edition of the Latin Bible, in 1456. Until that point in time, ordinary Christians had to rely on clergy to get access to the Scriptures that were the foundation of their faith. Now the door was opened to all people who desired to experience the Word of God for themselves. Universal literacy and education were also made possible, though not yet realities. The following decades brought printed editions of the Hebrew Old Testament, the Septuagint (a translation of the Hebrew Old Testament into Greek plus some additional books), and the Greek New Testament. The leaders of the Protestant Reformation were quick to take advantage of this new invention to help advance their efforts in Church reform.

4

 God's Love

And hope maketh not ashamed; because the love of God is shed abroad in our hearts by the Holy Ghost which is given unto us.

Romans 5:5

For the love of Christ constraineth us; because we thus judge, that if one died for all, then were all dead:

And that he died for all, that they which live should not henceforth live unto themselves, but unto him which died for them, and rose again.

2 Corinthians 5:14–15

For I am persuaded, that neither death, nor life, nor angels, nor principalities, nor powers, nor things present, nor things to come,

Nor height, nor depth, nor any other creature, shall be able to separate us from the love of God, which is in Christ Jesus our Lord.

Romans 8:38–39

Beloved, let us love one another: for love is of God; and every one that loveth is born of God, and knoweth God.

He that loveth not knoweth not God; for God is love.

In this was manifested the love of God toward us, because that God sent his only begotten Son into the world, that we might live through him.

1 John 4:7–9

Hereby perceive we the love of God, because he laid down his life for us: and we ought to lay down our lives for the brethren.

But whoso hath this world's good, and seeth his brother have need, and shutteth up his bowels of compassion from him, how dwelleth the love of God in him?

My little children, let us not love in word, neither in tongue; but in deed and in truth.

And hereby we know that we are of the truth, and shall assure our hearts before him.

1 John 3:16–19

But ye, beloved, building up yourselves on your most holy faith, praying in the Holy Ghost,

Keep yourselves in the love of God, looking for the mercy of our Lord Jesus Christ unto eternal life.

Jude 20–21

WHOSOEVER BELIEVETH that Jesus is the Christ is born of God: and every one that loveth him that begat loveth him also that is begotten of him.

By this we know that we love the children of God, when we love God, and keep his commandments.

For this is the love of God, that we keep his commandments: and his commandments are not grievous.

For whatsoever is born of God overcometh the world: and this is the victory that overcometh the world, even our faith.

1 John 5:1–4

But whoso keepeth his word, in him verily is the love of God perfected: hereby know we that we are in him.

1 John 2:5

God's Grace

For the Lord God is a sun and shield: the Lord will give grace and glory: no good thing will he withhold from them that walk uprightly.

Psalm 84:11

For this thing I besought the Lord thrice, that it might depart from me.

And he said unto me, My grace is sufficient for thee: for my strength is made perfect in weakness. Most gladly therefore will I rather glory in my infirmities, that the power of Christ may rest upon me.

Therefore I take pleasure in infirmities, in reproaches, in necessities, in persecutions, in distresses for Christ's sake: for when I am weak, then am I strong.

2 Corinthians 12:8–10

In whom we have redemption through his blood, the forgiveness of sins, according to the riches of his grace;

Wherein he hath abounded toward us in all wisdom and prudence.

Ephesians 1:7–8

Humble yourselves therefore under the mighty hand of God, that he may exalt you in due time:

Casting all your care upon him; for he careth for you.

Be sober, be vigilant; because your adversary the devil, as a roaring lion, walketh about, seeking whom he may devour:

Whom resist stedfast in the faith, knowing that the same afflictions are accomplished in your brethren that are in the world.

But the God of all grace, who hath called us unto his eternal glory by Christ Jesus, after that ye have suffered a while, make you perfect, stablish, strengthen, settle you.

1 Peter 5:6–10

For the grace of God that bringeth salvation hath appeared to all men,

Teaching us that, denying ungodliness and worldly lusts, we should live soberly, righteously, and godly, in this present world;

Looking for that blessed hope, and the glorious appearing of the great God and our Saviour Jesus Christ;

Who gave himself for us, that he might redeem us from all iniquity, and purify unto himself a peculiar people, zealous of good works.

Titus 2:11–14

Therefore, brethren, stand fast, and hold the traditions which ye have been taught, whether by word, or our epistle.

Now our Lord Jesus Christ himself, and God, even our Father, which hath loved us, and hath given us everlasting consolation and good hope through grace,

Comfort your hearts, and stablish you in every good word and work.

2 Thessalonians 2:15–17

But after that the kindness and love of God our Saviour toward man appeared,

Not by works of righteousness which we have done, but according to his mercy he saved us, by the washing of regeneration, and renewing of the Holy Ghost;

Which he shed on us abundantly through Jesus Christ our Saviour; that being justified by his grace, we should be made heirs according to the hope of eternal life.

Titus 3:4–7

But God, who is rich in mercy, for his great love wherewith he loved us. . . .

And hath raised us up together, and made us sit together in heavenly places in Christ Jesus:

That in the ages to come he might shew the exceeding riches of his grace in his kindness toward us through Christ Jesus. For by grace are ye saved through faith; and that not of yourselves: it is the gift of God.

Ephesians 2:4, 6–8

God's Spirit

So then they that are in the flesh cannot please God.

But ye are not in the flesh, but in the Spirit, if so be that the Spirit of God dwell in you. Now if any man have not the Spirit of Christ, he is none of his.

And if Christ be in you, the body is dead because of sin; but the Spirit is life because of righteousness.

But if the Spirit of him that raised up Jesus from the dead dwell in you, he that raised up Christ from the dead shall also quicken your mortal bodies by his Spirit that dwelleth in you.

Romans 8:8–11

BELOVED, BELIEVE not every spirit, but try the spirits whether they are of God: because many false prophets are gone out into the world.

Hereby know ye the Spirit of God: Every spirit that confesseth that Jesus Christ is come in the flesh is of God:

And every spirit that confesseth not that Jesus Christ is come in the flesh is not of God.

1 John 4:1–3

But as it is written, Eye hath not seen, nor ear heard, neither have entered into the heart of man, the things which God hath prepared for them that love him.

But God hath revealed them unto us by his Spirit: for the Spirit searcheth all things, yea, the deep things of God.

For what man knoweth the things of a man, save the spirit of man which is in him? even so the things of God knoweth no man, but the Spirit of God.

Now we have received, not the spirit of the world, but the spirit which is of God; that we might know the things that are freely given to us of God.

1 Corinthians 2:9–12

Nevertheless, when it shall turn to the Lord, the vail shall be taken away.

Now the Lord is that Spirit: and where the Spirit of the Lord is, there is liberty.

But we all, with open face beholding as in a glass the glory of the Lord, are changed into the same image from glory to glory, even as by the Spirit of the Lord.

2 Corinthians 3:16–18

And Jesus, when he was baptized, went up straightway out of the water: and, lo, the heavens were opened unto him, and he saw the Spirit of God descending like a dove, and lighting upon him.

Matthew 3:16

Know ye not that ye are the temple of God, and that the Spirit of God dwelleth in you?

If any man defile the temple of God, him shall God destroy; for the temple of God is holy, which temple ye are.

1 Corinthians 3:16–17

THE SPIRIT of the Lord GOD is upon me; because the LORD hath anointed me to preach good tidings unto the meek; he hath sent me to bind up the brokenhearted, to proclaim liberty to the captives, and the opening of the prison to them that are bound;

To proclaim the acceptable year of the LORD, and the day of vengeance of our God; to comfort all that mourn;

To appoint unto them that mourn in Zion, to give unto them beauty for ashes, the oil of joy for mourning, the garment of praise for the spirit of heaviness; that they might be called trees of righteousness, the planting of the LORD, that he might be glorified.

Isaiah 61:1–3

God's Compassion

But thou, O Lord, art a God full of compassion, and gracious, longsuffering, and plenteous in mercy and truth.

O turn unto me, and have mercy upon me; give thy strength unto thy servant, and save the son of thine handmaid.

Psalm 86:15–16

But he, being full of compassion, forgave their iniquity, and destroyed them not: yea, many a time turned he his anger away, and did not stir up all his wrath.

For he remembered that they were but flesh; a wind that passeth away, and cometh not again.

Psalm 78:38–39

The Lord is gracious, and full of compassion; slow to anger, and of great mercy.

The Lord is good to all: and his tender mercies are over all his works.

Psalm 145:8–9

And Jesus went about all the cities and villages, teaching in their synagogues, and preaching the gospel of the kingdom, and healing every sickness and every disease among the people.

But when he saw the multitudes, he was moved with compassion on them, because they fainted, and were scattered abroad, as sheep having no shepherd.

Then saith he unto his disciples, The harvest truly is plenteous, but the labourers are few; pray ye therefore the Lord of the harvest, that he will send forth labourers into his harvest.

Matthew 9:35–38

What shall we say then? Is there unrighteousness with God? God forbid.

For he saith to Moses, I will have mercy on whom I will have mercy, and I will have compassion on whom I will have compassion.

So then it is not of him that willeth, nor of him that runneth, but of God that sheweth mercy.

Romans 9:14–16

Who is a God like unto thee, that pardoneth iniquity, and passeth by the transgression of the remnant of his heritage? he retaineth not his anger for ever, because he delighteth in mercy.

He will turn again, he will have compassion upon us; he will subdue our iniquities; and thou wilt cast all their sins into the depths of the sea.

Micah 7:18–19

And there came a leper to him, beseeching him, and kneeling down to him, and saying unto him, If thou wilt, thou canst make me clean.

And Jesus, moved with compassion, put forth his hand, and touched him, and saith unto him, I WILL; BE THOU CLEAN.

Mark 1:40–41

Finally, be ye all of one mind, having compassion one of another, love as brethren, be pitiful, be courteous:

Not rendering evil for evil, or railing for railing: but contrariwise blessing; knowing that ye are thereunto called, that ye should inherit a blessing.

1 Peter 3:8–9

God's Mercy

O give thanks unto the LORD; for he is good;
for his mercy endureth for ever.

1 Chronicles 16:34

And when he had consulted with the people, he
appointed singers unto the LORD, and that should
praise the beauty of holiness, as they went out before
the army, and to say,
　"Praise the LORD;
for his mercy endureth for ever."

2 Chronicles 20:21

PRAISE YE the LORD. O give thanks unto the LORD; for
he is good: for his mercy endureth for ever.
　Who can utter the mighty acts of the LORD? who can
shew forth all his praise?
　Blessed are they that keep judgment, and he that
doeth righteousness at all times.

Psalm 106:1–3

For he saith to Moses, I will have mercy on whom I will have mercy, and I will have compassion on whom I will have compassion.

So then it is not of him that willeth, nor of him that runneth, but of God that sheweth mercy.

Romans 9:15–16

As concerning the gospel, they are enemies for your sakes: but as touching the election, they are beloved for the fathers' sakes.

For the gifts and calling of God are without repentance.

For as ye in times past have not believed God, yet have now obtained mercy through their unbelief: even so have these also now not believed, that through your mercy they also may obtain mercy.

For God hath concluded them all in unbelief, that he might have mercy upon all.

Romans 11:28–32

Have mercy upon me, O God, according to thy lovingkindness: according unto the multitude of thy tender mercies blot out my transgressions.

Wash me throughly from mine iniquity, and cleanse me from my sin.

Psalm 51:1–2

O GIVE thanks unto the Lord, for he is good: for his mercy endureth for ever.

Let the redeemed of the Lord say so, whom he hath redeemed from the hand of the enemy;

And gathered them out of the lands, from the east, and from the west, from the north, and from the south.

Psalm 107:1–3

O GIVE thanks unto the Lord; for he is good: because his mercy endureth for ever.

Let Israel now say, that his mercy endureth for ever.

Let the house of Aaron now say, that his mercy endureth for ever.

Let them now that fear the Lord say, that his mercy endureth for ever.

Psalm 118:1–4

The Apocrypha of the King James Version

The English-language King James Version of 1611 followed the lead of the Luther Bible in using an inter-testamental section labelled "Books called Apocrypha."

All English translations of the Bible printed in the sixteenth century included a section or appendix for Apocryphal books. Matthew's Bible, published in 1537, contains all the Apocrypha of the later King James Version in an inter-testamental section. The 1538 Myles Coverdale Bible contained an Apocrypha which excluded Baruch and the Prayer of Manasseh. The 1560 Geneva Bible placed the Prayer of Manasseh after 2 Chronicles; the rest of the Apocrypha were placed in an inter-testamental section. The Douay-Rheims Bible (1582–1609) placed the Prayer of Manasseh and 3 and 4 Esdras into an Appendix of the second volume of the Old Testament.

All King James Bibles published before 1640 included the Apocrypha. In 1826, the British and Foreign Bible Society decided that no BFBS funds were to pay for printing any Apocryphal books anywhere. Since then most modern editions of the Bible and re-printings of the King James Bible omit the Apocrypha section. In the 18th century, the Apocrypha section was omitted from the Challoner revision of the Douay-Rheims version. In the 1979 revision of the

Vulgate, the section was dropped. Modern reprintings of the Clementine Vulgate commonly omit the Apocrypha section. Many reprintings of older versions of the Bible now omit the apocrypha and many newer translations and revisions have never included them at all.

There are some exceptions to this trend, however. Some editions of the Revised Standard Version of the Bible include not only the Apocrypha listed above, but also the third and fourth books of the Maccabees, and Psalm 151; the RSV Apocrypha also lists the Letter of Jeremiah (Epistle of Jeremy in the KJV) as separate from the book of Baruch, following the Orthodox tradition.

The American Bible Society lifted restrictions on the publication of Bibles with the Apocrypha in 1964. The British and Foreign Bible Society followed in 1966. The Stuttgart edition of the Vulgate (the printed edition, not most of the on-line editions), which is published by the UBS, contains the Clementine Apocrypha, as well as the Epistle to the Laodiceans and Psalm 151.

God's Faithfulness

Thy mercy, O LORD, is in the heavens; and thy faithfulness reacheth unto the clouds.

Thy righteousness is like the great mountains; thy judgments are a great deep: O LORD, thou preservest man and beast.

How excellent is thy lovingkindness, O God! therefore the children of men put their trust under the shadow of thy wings.

Psalm 36:5–7

Let us draw near with a true heart in full assurance of faith, having our hearts sprinkled from an evil conscience, and our bodies washed with pure water.

Let us hold fast the profession of our faith without wavering; (for he is faithful that promised;) and let us consider one another to provoke unto love and to good works.

Hebrews 10:22–24

I will sing of the mercies of the LORD for ever: with my mouth will I make known thy faithfulness to all generations.

For I have said, Mercy shall be built up for ever: thy faithfulness shalt thou establish in the very heavens.

Psalm 89:1–2

And the very God of peace sanctify you wholly; and I pray God your whole spirit and soul and body be preserved blameless unto the coming of our Lord Jesus Christ. Faithful is he that calleth you, who also will do it.

1 Thessalonians 5:23–24

For ever, O LORD, thy word is settled in heaven.

Thy faithfulness is unto all generations: thou hast established the earth, and it abideth.

They continue this day according to thine ordinances: for all are thy servants.

Psalm 119:89–91

It is of the LORD's mercies that we are not consumed, because his compassions fail not.

They are new every morning: great is thy faithfulness.

The LORD is my portion, saith my soul; therefore will I hope in him.

Lamentations 3:22–24

It is a good thing to give thanks unto the LORD, and to sing praises unto thy name, O most High:

To shew forth thy lovingkindness in the morning, and thy faithfulness every night,

Upon an instrument of ten strings, and upon the psaltery; upon the harp with a solemn sound.

For thou, LORD, hast made me glad through thy work: I will triumph in the works of thy hands.

Psalm 92:1-4

There hath no temptation taken you but such as is common to man: but God is faithful, who will not suffer you to be tempted above that ye are able; but will with the temptation also make a way to escape, that ye may be able to bear it.

1 Corinthians 10:13

God's Kindness

Blessed be the LORD: for he hath shewed me his marvellous kindness in a strong city. . . .

O love the LORD, all ye his saints: for the LORD preserveth the faithful, and plentifully rewardeth the proud doer.

Be of good courage, and he shall strengthen your heart, all ye that hope in the LORD.

Psalm 31:21, 23–24

O praise the LORD, all ye nations: praise him, all ye people.

For his merciful kindness is great toward us: and the truth of the LORD endureth for ever. Praise ye the LORD.

Psalm 117:1–2

For the mountains shall depart, and the hills be removed; but my kindness shall not depart from thee, neither shall the covenant of my peace be removed, saith the LORD that hath mercy on thee.

Isaiah 54:10

For we ourselves also were sometimes foolish, disobedient, deceived, serving divers lusts and pleasures, living in malice and envy, hateful, and hating one another.

But after that the kindness and love of God our Saviour toward man appeared,

Not by works of righteousness which we have done, but according to his mercy he saved us, by the washing of regeneration, and renewing of the Holy Ghost;

Which he shed on us abundantly through Jesus Christ our Saviour;

That being justified by his grace, we should be made heirs according to the hope of eternal life.

Titus 3:3–7

And beside this, giving all diligence, add to your faith virtue; and to virtue knowledge;

And to knowledge temperance; and to temperance patience; and to patience godliness;

And to godliness brotherly kindness; and to brotherly kindness charity.

For if these things be in you, and abound, they make you that ye shall neither be barren nor unfruitful in the knowledge of our Lord Jesus Christ.

2 Peter 1:5–8

But love ye your enemies, and do good, and lend, hoping for nothing again; and your reward shall be great, and ye shall be the children of the Highest: for he is kind unto the unthankful and to the evil.

Be ye therefore merciful, as your Father also is merciful.

Luke 6:35–36

Let all bitterness, and wrath, and anger, and clamour, and evil speaking, be put away from you, with all malice:

And be ye kind one to another, tenderhearted, forgiving one another, even as God for Christ's sake hath forgiven you.

Ephesians 4:31–32

Let love be without dissimulation. Abhor that which is evil; cleave to that which is good.

Be kindly affectioned one to another with brotherly love; in honour preferring one another;

Not slothful in business; fervent in spirit; serving the Lord;

Rejoicing in hope; patient in tribulation; continuing instant in prayer;

Distributing to the necessity of saints; given to hospitality.

Romans 12:9–13

God's Patience

For whatsoever things were written aforetime were written for our learning, that we through patience and comfort of the scriptures might have hope.

Now the God of patience and consolation grant you to be likeminded one toward another according to Christ Jesus:

That ye may with one mind and one mouth glorify God, even the Father of our Lord Jesus Christ.

Romans 15:4–6

And we beseech you, brethren, to know them which labour among you, and are over you in the Lord, and admonish you;

And to esteem them very highly in love for their work's sake. And be at peace among yourselves.

Now we exhort you, brethren, warn them that are unruly, comfort the feebleminded, support the weak, be patient toward all men.

1 Thessalonians 5:12–14

My brethren, count it all joy when ye fall into divers temptations;

Knowing this, that the trying of your faith worketh patience.

But let patience have her perfect work, that ye may be perfect and entire, wanting nothing.

James 1:2–4

But thou, O man of God, flee these things; and follow after righteousness, godliness, faith, love, patience, meekness.

Fight the good fight of faith, lay hold on eternal life, whereunto thou art also called, and hast professed a good profession before many witnesses.

I give thee charge in the sight of God, who quickeneth all things, and before Christ Jesus, who before Pontius Pilate witnessed a good confession;

That thou keep this commandment without spot, unrebukeable, until the appearing of our Lord Jesus Christ.

1 Timothy 6:11–14

Rest in the LORD, and wait patiently for him: fret not thyself because of him who prospereth in his way, because of the man who bringeth wicked devices to pass.

Cease from anger, and forsake wrath: fret not thyself in any wise to do evil.

Psalm 37:7–8

For God is not unrighteous to forget your work and labour of love, which ye have shewed toward his name, in that ye have ministered to the saints, and do minister.

And we desire that every one of you do shew the same diligence to the full assurance of hope unto the end:

That ye be not slothful, but followers of them who through faith and patience inherit the promises.

Hebrews 6:10–12

Be patient therefore, brethren, unto the coming of the Lord. Behold, the husbandman waiteth for the precious fruit of the earth, and hath long patience for it, until he receive the early and latter rain.

Be ye also patient; stablish your hearts: for the coming of the Lord draweth nigh.

James 5:7–8

Let love be without dissimulation. Abhor that which is evil; cleave to that which is good.

Be kindly affectioned one to another with brotherly love; in honour preferring one another;

Not slothful in business; fervent in spirit; serving the Lord;

Rejoicing in hope; patient in tribulation; continuing instant in prayer.

Romans 12:9–12

God's Forgiveness

Bless the LORD, O my soul: and all that is within me, bless his holy name.

Bless the LORD, O my soul, and forget not all his benefits:

Who forgiveth all thine iniquities; who healeth all thy diseases;

Who redeemeth thy life from destruction; who crowneth thee with lovingkindness and tender mercies.

Psalm 103:1–4

The LORD is merciful and gracious, slow to anger, and plenteous in mercy.

He will not always chide: neither will he keep his anger for ever.

He hath not dealt with us after our sins; nor rewarded us according to our iniquities.

For as the heaven is high above the earth, so great is his mercy toward them that fear him.

As far as the east is from the west, so far hath he removed our transgressions from us.

Psalm 103:8–12

In whom also ye are circumcised with the circumcision made without hands, in putting off the body of the sins of the flesh by the circumcision of Christ:

Buried with him in baptism, wherein also ye are risen with him through the faith of the operation of God, who hath raised him from the dead.

And you, being dead in your sins and the uncircumcision of your flesh, hath he quickened together with him, having forgiven you all trespasses;

Blotting out the handwriting of ordinances that was against us, which was contrary to us, and took it out of the way, nailing it to his cross.

Colossians 2:11–14

If we say that we have no sin, we deceive ourselves, and the truth is not in us.

If we confess our sins, he is faithful and just to forgive us our sins, and to cleanse us from all unrighteousness.

1 John 1:8–9

Lord, hear my voice: let thine ears be attentive to the voice of my supplications.

If thou, LORD, shouldest mark iniquities, O Lord, who shall stand?

But there is forgiveness with thee, that thou mayest be feared.

I wait for the LORD, my soul doth wait, and in his word do I hope.

Psalm 130:2–5

In whom we have redemption through his blood, the forgiveness of sins, according to the riches of his grace;

Wherein he hath abounded toward us in all wisdom and prudence;

Having made known unto us the mystery of his will, according to his good pleasure which he hath purposed in himself:

That in the dispensation of the fulness of times he might gather together in one all things in Christ, both which are in heaven, and which are on earth; even in him.

Ephesians 1:7–10

If my people, which are called by my name, shall humble themselves, and pray, and seek my face, and turn from their wicked ways; then will I hear from heaven, and will forgive their sin, and will heal their land.

2 Chronicles 7:14

Giving thanks unto the Father, which hath made us meet to be partakers of the inheritance of the saints in light:

Who hath delivered us from the power of darkness, and hath translated us into the kingdom of his dear Son:

In whom we have redemption through his blood, even the forgiveness of sins.

Colossians 1:12–14

I, even I, am he that blotteth out thy transgressions for mine own sake, and will not remember thy sins.

Isaiah 43:25

I acknowledged my sin unto thee, and mine iniquity have I not hid. I said, I will confess my transgressions unto the LORD; and thou forgavest the iniquity of my sin.

For this shall every one that is godly pray unto thee in a time when thou mayest be found: surely in the floods of great waters they shall not come nigh unto him.

Thou art my hiding place; thou shalt preserve me from trouble; thou shalt compass me about with songs of deliverance.

Psalm 32:5–7

God's Righteousness

    And if Christ be in you, the body is dead because of sin; but the Spirit is life because of righteousness.

    But if the Spirit of him that raised up Jesus from the dead dwell in you, he that raised up Christ from the dead shall also quicken your mortal bodies by his Spirit that dwelleth in you.

Romans 8:10–11

    Wherefore take unto you the whole armour of God, that ye may be able to withstand in the evil day, and having done all, to stand.

    Stand therefore, having your loins girt about with truth, and having on the breastplate of righteousness;

    And your feet shod with the preparation of the gospel of peace;

    Above all, taking the shield of faith, wherewith ye shall be able to quench all the fiery darts of the wicked.

    And take the helmet of salvation, and the sword of the Spirit, which is the word of God.

Ephesians 6:13–17

He that hath clean hands, and a pure heart; who hath not lifted up his soul unto vanity, nor sworn deceitfully.

He shall receive the blessing from the LORD, and righteousness from the God of his salvation.

Psalm 24:4–5

For if by one man's offence death reigned by one; much more they which receive abundance of grace and of the gift of righteousness shall reign in life by one, Jesus Christ.

Romans 5:17

For the righteous Lord loveth righteousness; his countenance doth behold the upright.

Psalm 11:7

He that walketh righteously, and speaketh uprightly; he that despiseth the gain of oppressions, that shaketh his hands from holding of bribes, that stoppeth his ears from hearing of blood, and shutteth his eyes from seeing evil;

He shall dwell on high: his place of defence shall be the munitions of rocks: bread shall be given him; his waters shall be sure.

Isaiah 33:15–16

The just man walketh in his integrity: his children are blessed after him.

Proverbs 20:7

A righteous man hateth lying: but a wicked man is loathsome, and cometh to shame.

Righteousness keepeth him that is upright in the way: but wickedness overthroweth the sinner.

Proverbs 13:5–6

Mercy and truth are met together; righteousness and peace have kissed each other.

Truth shall spring out of the earth; and righteousness shall look down from heaven.

Yea, the LORD shall give that which is good; and our land shall yield her increase.

Righteousness shall go before him; and shall set us in the way of his steps.

Psalm 85:10–13

The Translation Process

When King James announced the decision to undertake a new translation of the Bible, he appointed to the project 54 of the best biblical scholars and linguists of their day. The translation was to be a truly collaborative work. Furthermore, detailed guidelines were set forth for the translation process.

The group of scholars and linguists (numbering 47 by the time the translation was begun) was divided into six committees. Two committees would work at Oxford, two at Cambridge, and two in Westminster, and each committee was assigned books of the Bible to translate. Ten scholars at Westminster were assigned Genesis through 2 Kings; seven had Romans through Jude. At Cambridge, eight worked on 1 Chronicles through the Song of Solomon, while seven others handled the Apocrypha. Oxford employed seven to translate Isaiah through Malachi; eight occupied themselves with the Gospels, Acts, and Revelation.

In the preface to the 1611 edition, the translators of the King James Version state that it was not their purpose "to make a new translation, but to make a good one better, or out of many good ones one principle good one." Their translation effort was based primarily on the 1602 edition of the Bishops' Bible, but the translators also used the Tyndale,

Matthew, Coverdale, Great, Geneva, and Douay Bibles. The scholars were proficient in Hebrew and Greek and used the Masoretic text of the Complutensian Polyglot (1514–1517) for the Old Testament. For the New Testament they used the Textus Receptus published by Stephanus and Beza from 1550 onward.

The scholars readily appreciated the intrinsic beauty of divine revelation. The reason the King James Version is so rich in the nobility of its language is that the translators were careful to make it so. They disciplined their talents to render finely chosen English words of their time, as well as a graceful, often musical arrangement of language. The text was to be used at church services and read aloud, so the translators would read their versions aloud to one another and rewrite again and again to achieve the best emphasis of punctuation and the best rhythm in prose.

It took three years for the committees of scholars to complete the translation. Then, two scholars were selected for each committee to form a review committee of twelve, and three more years were spent reviewing and revising the work. Nicolson states that the end result was an astonishing document possessing "immediacy, dignity, a sense of deep, musical rhythm, an intuitive and poetic understanding of the connection between the present and the past, a tangible empathy, a precision . . . a careful elaboration of arrangement and structure."

After another nine months preparing the Bible for press, it was ready to be printed by the king's printer. The completed work was issued in 1611, the complete title page reading:

THE HOLY BIBLE,
Conteyning the Old Testament,
and the New:
Newly Translated out of the Originall tongues: & with
the former Translations diligently compared and
revised, by his Majesties Special Commandment.
Appointed to be read in Churches.
Imprinted at London by Robert Barker,
Printer to the Kings most Excellent Majestie.
ANNO DOM. 1611.

The King James Version was, in its first printing, 16" x 10 ½", which was even larger than the Great Bible. It was printed in black letter with small roman type to represent those words not in the original languages.

This version went through several editions and revisions. Two notable editions were that of 1629, the first ever printed at Cambridge, and that of 1638, also at Cambridge, which was assisted by John Bois and Samuel Ward, two of the original translators. The most important and permanent edition was the 1769 Oxford revision by Benjamin Blayney.

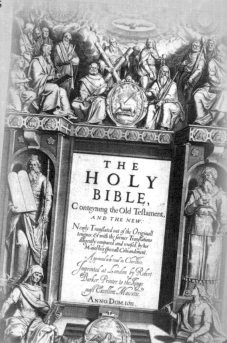

God's Comfort

Unless the LORD had been my help, my soul had almost dwelt in silence.

When I said, My foot slippeth; thy mercy, O LORD, held me up.

In the multitude of my thoughts within me thy comforts delight my soul.

Psalm 94:17–19

This is my comfort in my affliction: for thy word hath quickened me.

The proud have had me greatly in derision: yet have I not declined from thy law.

I remembered thy judgments of old, O LORD; and have comforted myself.

Psalm 119:50–52

Fear thou not; for I am with thee: be not dismayed; for I am thy God: I will strengthen thee; yea, I will help thee; yea, I will uphold thee with the right hand of my righteousness.

Isaiah 41:10

COMFORT YE, comfort ye my people, saith your God.

Speak ye comfortably to Jerusalem, and cry unto her, that her warfare is accomplished, that her iniquity is pardoned: for she hath received of the LORD's hand double for all her sins. . . .

Every valley shall be exalted, and every mountain and hill shall be made low: and the crooked shall be made straight, and the rough places plain:

And the glory of the LORD shall be revealed, and all flesh shall see it together: for the mouth of the LORD hath spoken it.

Isaiah 40:1–2, 4–5

Nevertheless God, that comforteth those that are cast down, comforted us by the coming of Titus;

And not by his coming only, but by the consolation wherewith he was comforted in you, when he told us your earnest desire, your mourning, your fervent mind toward me; so that I rejoiced the more.

2 Corinthians 7:6–7

Thou shalt increase my greatness, and comfort me on every side.

I will also praise thee with the psaltery, even thy truth, O my God: unto thee will I sing with the harp, O thou Holy One of Israel.

My lips shall greatly rejoice when I sing unto thee; and my soul, which thou hast redeemed.

Psalm 71:21–23

Blessed be God, even the Father of our Lord Jesus Christ, the Father of mercies, and the God of all comfort;

Who comforteth us in all our tribulation, that we may be able to comfort them which are in any trouble, by the comfort wherewith we ourselves are comforted of God.

For as the sufferings of Christ abound in us, so our consolation also aboundeth by Christ.

And whether we be afflicted, it is for your consolation and salvation, which is effectual in the enduring of the same sufferings which we also suffer: or whether we be comforted, it is for your consolation and salvation.

And our hope of you is stedfast, knowing, that as ye are partakers of the sufferings, so shall ye be also of the consolation.

2 Corinthians 1:3–7

Let, I pray thee, thy merciful kindness be for my comfort, according to thy word unto thy servant.

Let thy tender mercies come unto me, that I may live: for thy law is my delight.

Psalm 119:76–77

God's Power

Hast thou not known? hast thou not heard, that the everlasting God, the LORD, the Creator of the ends of the earth, fainteth not, neither is weary? there is no searching of his understanding.

He giveth power to the faint; and to them that have no might he increaseth strength.

Even the youths shall faint and be weary, and the young men shall utterly fall:

But they that wait upon the LORD shall renew their strength; they shall mount up with wings as eagles; they shall run, and not be weary; and they shall walk, and not faint.

Isaiah 40:28–31

Believe me that I am in the Father, and the Father in me: or else believe me for the very works' sake.

Verily, verily, I say unto you, He that believeth on me, the works that I do shall he do also; and greater works than these shall he do; because I go unto my Father.

And whatsoever ye shall ask in my name, that will I do, that the Father may be glorified in the Son.

John 14:11–13

And he said unto them, It is not for you to know the times or the seasons, which the Father hath put in his own power.

But ye shall receive power, after that the Holy Ghost is come upon you: and ye shall be witnesses unto me both in Jerusalem, and in all Judaea, and in Samaria, and unto the uttermost part of the earth.

Acts 1:7–8

For this thing I besought the Lord thrice, that it might depart from me.

And he said unto me, My grace is sufficient for thee: for my strength is made perfect in weakness. Most gladly therefore will I rather glory in my infirmities, that the power of Christ may rest upon me.

Therefore I take pleasure in infirmities, in reproaches, in necessities, in persecutions, in distresses for Christ's sake: for when I am weak, then am I strong.

2 Corinthians 12:8–10

So then it is not of him that willeth, nor of him that runneth, but of God that sheweth mercy.

For the scripture saith unto Pharaoh, Even for this same purpose have I raised thee up, that I might shew my power in thee, and that my name might be declared throughout all the earth.

Romans 9:16–17

Wherefore I desire that ye faint not at my tribulations for you, which is your glory.

For this cause I bow my knees unto the Father of our Lord Jesus Christ,

Of whom the whole family in heaven and earth is named,

That he would grant you, according to the riches of his glory, to be strengthened with might by his Spirit in the inner man; . . .

Now unto him that is able to do exceeding abundantly above all that we ask or think, according to the power that worketh in us,

Unto him be glory in the church by Christ Jesus throughout all ages, world without end. Amen.

Ephesians 3:13–16, 20–21

And my speech and my preaching was not with enticing words of man's wisdom, but in demonstration of the Spirit and of power:

That your faith should not stand in the wisdom of men, but in the power of God.

1 Corinthians 2:4–5

For God, who commanded the light to shine out of darkness, hath shined in our hearts, to give the light of the knowledge of the glory of God in the face of Jesus Christ.

But we have this treasure in earthen vessels, that the excellency of the power may be of God, and not of us.

2 Corinthians 4:6–7

God's Strength

I can do all things through Christ which strengtheneth me.

Philippians 4:13

The LORD is my strength and my shield; my heart trusted in him, and I am helped: therefore my heart greatly rejoiceth; and with my song will I praise him.

The LORD is their strength, and he is the saving strength of his anointed.

Save thy people, and bless thine inheritance: feed them also, and lift them up for ever.

Psalm 28:7–9

Trust ye in the Lord for ever: for in the Lord JEHOVAH is everlasting strength.

Isaiah 26:4

Give unto the LORD, O ye mighty, give unto the LORD glory and strength.

Give unto the LORD the glory due unto his name; worship the LORD in the beauty of holiness.

The voice of the LORD is upon the waters: the God of glory thundereth: the LORD is upon many waters.

The voice of the LORD is powerful; the voice of the LORD is full of majesty. . . .

The voice of the LORD maketh the hinds to calve, and discovereth the forests: and in his temple doth every one speak of his glory.

The LORD sitteth upon the flood; yea, the LORD sitteth King for ever.

The LORD will give strength unto his people; the LORD will bless his people with peace.

Psalm 29:1–4, 9–11

God is our refuge and strength, a very present help in trouble.

Therefore will not we fear, though the earth be removed, and though the mountains be carried into the midst of the sea;

Though the waters thereof roar and be troubled, though the mountains shake with the swelling thereof.

There is a river, the streams whereof shall make glad the city of God, the holy place of the tabernacles of the most High.

God is in the midst of her; she shall not be moved: God shall help her, and that right early.

Psalm 46:1–5

Whom have I in heaven but thee? and there is none upon earth that I desire beside thee.

My flesh and my heart faileth: but God is the strength of my heart, and my portion for ever.

For, lo, they that are far from thee shall perish: thou hast destroyed all them that go a whoring from thee.

But it is good for me to draw near to God: I have put my trust in the Lord God, that I may declare all thy works.

Psalm 73:25–28

And he said unto me, My grace is sufficient for thee: for my strength is made perfect in weakness. Most gladly therefore will I rather glory in my infirmities, that the power of Christ may rest upon me.

Therefore I take pleasure in infirmities, in reproaches, in necessities, in persecutions, in distresses for Christ's sake: for when I am weak, then am I strong.

2 Corinthians 12:9–10

Fear thou not; for I am with thee: be not dismayed; for I am thy God: I will strengthen thee; yea, I will help thee; yea, I will uphold thee with the right hand of my righteousness.

Isaiah 41:10

God's Presence

They that trust in the Lord shall be as mount Zion, which cannot be removed, but abideth for ever.

As the mountains are round about Jerusalem, so the Lord is round about his people from henceforth even for ever.

Psalm 125:1–2

A new heart also will I give you, and a new spirit will I put within you: and I will take away the stony heart out of your flesh, and I will give you an heart of flesh.

And I will put my spirit within you, and cause you to walk in my statutes, and ye shall keep my judgments, and do them.

And ye shall dwell in the land that I gave to your fathers; and ye shall be my people, and I will be your God.

Ezekiel 36:26–28

Thou hast made known to me the ways of life; thou shalt make me full of joy with thy countenance.

Acts 2:28

What shall we then say to these things? If God be for us, who can be against us?

He that spared not his own Son, but delivered him up for us all, how shall he not with him also freely give us all things?

Who shall lay any thing to the charge of God's elect? It is God that justifieth.

Who is he that condemneth? It is Christ that died, yea rather, that is risen again, who is even at the right hand of God, who also maketh intercession for us.

Who shall separate us from the love of Christ? shall tribulation, or distress, or persecution, or famine, or nakedness, or peril, or sword?

As it is written, For thy sake we are killed all the day long; we are accounted as sheep for the slaughter.

Nay, in all these things we are more than conquerors through him that loved us.

For I am persuaded, that neither death, nor life, nor angels, nor principalities, nor powers, nor things present, nor things to come,

Nor height, nor depth, nor any other creature, shall be able to separate us from the love of God, which is in Christ Jesus our Lord.

Romans 8:31–39

Be strong and of a good courage, fear not, nor be afraid of them: for the Lord thy God, he it is that doth go with thee; he will not fail thee, nor forsake thee.

Deuteronomy 31:6

I have set the LORD always before me: because he is at my right hand, I shall not be moved.

Therefore my heart is glad, and my glory rejoiceth: my flesh also shall rest in hope. . . .

Thou wilt shew me the path of life: in thy presence is fulness of joy; at thy right hand there are pleasures for evermore.

Psalm 16:8–9, 11

I know that the LORD will maintain the cause of the afflicted, and the right of the poor.

Surely the righteous shall give thanks unto thy name: the upright shall dwell in thy presence.

Psalm 140:12–13

For Christ is not entered into the holy places made with hands, which are the figures of the true; but into heaven itself, now to appear in the presence of God for us.

Hebrews 9:24

God's Blessings

The lips of the righteous feed many: but fools die for want of wisdom.

The blessing of the Lord, it maketh rich, and he addeth no sorrow with it.

Proverbs 10:21–22

A faithful man shall abound with blessings: but he that maketh haste to be rich shall not be innocent.

Proverbs 28:20

Thus saith the Lord, As the new wine is found in the cluster, and one saith, Destroy it not; for a blessing is in it: so will I do for my servants' sakes, that I may not destroy them all.

And I will bring forth a seed out of Jacob, and out of Judah an inheritor of my mountains: and mine elect shall inherit it, and my servants shall dwell there.

And Sharon shall be a fold of flocks, and the valley of Achor a place for the herds to lie down in, for my people that have sought me.

Isaiah 65:8–10

Bring ye all the tithes into the storehouse, that there may be meat in mine house, and prove me now herewith, saith the Lord of hosts, if I will not open you the windows of heaven, and pour you out a blessing, that there shall not be room enough to receive it.

Malachi 3:10

Nevertheless the Lord thy God would not hearken unto Balaam; but the Lord thy God turned the curse into a blessing unto thee, because the Lord thy God loved thee.

Deuteronomy 23:5

Bless the Lord, O my soul: and all that is within me, bless his holy name.

Bless the Lord, O my soul, and forget not all his benefits:

Who forgiveth all thine iniquities; who healeth all thy diseases;

Who redeemeth thy life from destruction; who crowneth thee with lovingkindness and tender mercies;

Who satisfieth thy mouth with good things; so that thy youth is renewed like the eagle's.

Psalm 103:1–5

Blessed be the Lord, who daily loadeth us with benefits, even the God of our salvation.

Psalm 68:19

Blessed be the LORD: for he hath shewed me his marvellous kindness in a strong city.

For I said in my haste, I am cut off from before thine eyes: nevertheless thou heardest the voice of my supplications when I cried unto thee.

O love the LORD, all ye his saints: for the LORD preserveth the faithful, and plentifully rewardeth the proud doer.

Be of good courage, and he shall strengthen your heart, all ye that hope in the LORD.

Psalm 31:21–24

Blessed be the LORD my strength, which teacheth my hands to war, and my fingers to fight:

My goodness, and my fortress; my high tower, and my deliverer; my shield, and he in whom I trust; who subdueth my people under me.

Psalm 144:1–2

1638 King James Revision

For most of the seventeenth century the assumption remained that, while it had been of vital importance to provide the Scriptures in the vernacular for ordinary people, nevertheless for those with sufficient education to do so, Biblical study was best undertaken within the international common medium of Latin. It was only in 1700 that modern bilingual Bibles appeared in which the Authorized Version was compared with counterpart Dutch and French Protestant vernacular Bibles.

In consequence of the continual disputes over printing privileges, successive printings of the Authorized Version were notably less careful than the 1611 edition had been—compositors freely varying spelling, capitalization, and punctuation—and also, over the years, introducing about 1,500 misprints (some of which, like the omission of "not" from the commandment "Thou shalt not commit adultery" in the "Wicked Bible," became notorious). The two Cambridge editions of 1629 and 1638 attempted to restore the proper text—while introducing over 200 revisions of the original translators' work, chiefly by incorporating into the main text a more literal reading originally presented as a marginal note. A more thoroughly corrected edition was proposed following the Restoration, in conjunction with the revised 1662 *Book of Common Prayer*, but Parliament then decided against it.

By the first half of the eighteenth century, the Authorized Version was effectively unchallenged as the sole English translation in current use in Protestant churches. It was so dominant that the Roman Catholic Church in England issued in 1750 a revision of the 1610 *Douay-Rheims Bible* by Richard Challoner that was very much closer to the Authorized Version than to the original. However, general standards of spelling, punctuation, typesetting, capitalization, and grammar had changed radically in the 100 years since the first edition of the Authorized Version, and all printers in the market were introducing continual piecemeal changes to their Bible texts to bring them into line with current practice—and with public expectations of standardized spelling and grammatical construction.

Over the course of the eighteenth century, the Authorized Version supplanted the Latin Vulgate as the standard version of Scripture for Englishspeaking scholars and divines, and indeed came to be regarded by some as an inspired text in itself—so much so that any challenge to its readings or textual base came to be regarded by many as an assault on Holy Scripture. A key milestone in this process was the publication in 1737 of *Alexander Cruden's Complete Concordance to the Holy Scriptures*, in which the English words of the Authorized Version were analyzed with no regard to the original tongues.

God's Peace

Open ye the gates, that the righteous nation which keepeth the truth may enter in.

Thou wilt keep him in perfect peace, whose mind is stayed on thee: because he trusteth in thee.

Trust ye in the LORD for ever: for in the LORD JEHOVAH is everlasting strength.

Isaiah 26:2–4

These things I have spoken unto you, that in me ye might have peace. In the world ye shall have tribulation: but be of good cheer; I have overcome the world.

John 16:33

Therefore being justified by faith, we have peace with God through our Lord Jesus Christ:

By whom also we have access by faith into this grace wherein we stand, and rejoice in hope of the glory of God.

Romans 5:1–2

And let the peace of God rule in your hearts, to the which also ye are called in one body; and be ye thankful.

Colossians 3:15

Peace I leave with you, my peace I give unto you: not as the world giveth, give I unto you. Let not your heart be troubled, neither let it be afraid.

Ye have heard how I said unto you, I go away, and come again unto you. If ye loved me, ye would rejoice, because I said, I go unto the Father: for my Father is greater than I.

John 14:27–28

For he is our peace, who hath made both one, and hath broken down the middle wall of partition between us;

Having abolished in his flesh the enmity, even the law of commandments contained in ordinances; for to make in himself of twain one new man, so making peace.

Ephesians 2:14–15

Finally, brethren, farewell. Be perfect, be of good comfort, be of one mind, live in peace; and the God of love and peace shall be with you.

2 Corinthians 13:11

For unto us a child is born, unto us a son is given: and the government shall be upon his shoulder: and his name shall be called Wonderful, Counsellor, The mighty God, The everlasting Father, The Prince of Peace.

Isaiah 9:6

Through the tender mercy of our God; whereby the dayspring from on high hath visited us,

To give light to them that sit in darkness and in the shadow of death, to guide our feet into the way of peace.

Luke 1:78–79

God's Guidance

Thus saith the LORD, thy Redeemer, the Holy One of Israel; I am the LORD thy God which teacheth thee to profit, which leadeth thee by the way that thou shouldest go.

Isaiah 48:17

Commit thy works unto the LORD, and thy thoughts shall be established.

Proverbs 16:3

And the LORD shall guide thee continually, and satisfy thy soul in drought, and make fat thy bones: and thou shalt be like a watered garden, and like a spring of water, whose waters fail not.

Isaiah 58:11

I the LORD have called thee in righteousness, and will hold thine hand, and will keep thee, and give thee for a covenant of the people, for a light of the Gentiles.

Isaiah 42:6

Trust in the LORD with all thine heart; and lean not unto thine own understanding.

In all thy ways acknowledge him, and he shall direct thy paths.

Proverbs 3:5–6

And I will put my spirit within you, and cause you to walk in my statutes, and ye shall keep my judgments, and do them.

Ezekiel 36:27

Howbeit when he, the Spirit of truth, is come, he will guide you into all truth: for he shall not speak of himself; but whatsoever he shall hear, that shall he speak: and he will shew you things to come.

John 16:13

For this God is our God for ever and ever: he will be our guide even unto death.

Psalm 48:14

I will instruct thee and teach thee in the way which thou shalt go: I will guide thee with mine eye.

Psalm 32:8

God's Wisdom

He that hath my commandments, and keepeth them, he it is that loveth me: and he that loveth me shall be loved of my Father, and I will love him, and will manifest myself to him.

John 14:21

In thee, O Lord, do I put my trust; let me never be ashamed: deliver me in thy righteousness.

Bow down thine ear to me; deliver me speedily: be thou my strong rock, for an house of defence to save me.

For thou art my rock and my fortress; therefore for thy name's sake lead me, and guide me.

Pull me out of the net that they have laid privily for me: for thou art my strength.

Into thine hand I commit my spirit: thou hast redeemed me, O Lord God of truth.

Psalm 31:1–5

Deal with thy servant according unto thy mercy, and teach me thy statutes.

I am thy servant; give me understanding, that I may know thy testimonies.

Psalm 119:124–125

Abide in me, and I in you. As the branch cannot bear fruit of itself, except it abide in the vine; no more can ye, except ye abide in me.

I am the vine, ye are the branches: He that abideth in me, and I in him, the same bringeth forth much fruit: for without me ye can do nothing.

If a man abide not in me, he is cast forth as a branch, and is withered; and men gather them, and cast them into the fire, and they are burned.

If ye abide in me, and my words abide in you, ye shall ask what ye will, and it shall be done unto you.

John 15:4–7

FOR I would that ye knew what great conflict I have for you, and for them at Laodicea, and for as many as have not seen my face in the flesh;

That their hearts might be comforted, being knit together in love, and unto all riches of the full assurance of understanding, to the acknowledgement of the mystery of God, and of the Father, and of Christ;

In whom are hid all the treasures of wisdom and knowledge.

Colossians 2:1–3

Unto me, who am less than the least of all saints,
is this grace given, that I should preach among the
Gentiles the unsearchable riches of Christ;

And to make all men see what is the fellowship of the
mystery, which from the beginning of the world hath
been hid in God, who created all things by Jesus Christ:

To the intent that now unto the principalities and
powers in heavenly places might be known by the
church the manifold wisdom of God.

Ephesians 3:8–10

MY SON, if thou wilt receive my words, and hide my
commandments with thee;

So that thou incline thine ear unto wisdom, and
apply thine heart to understanding;

Yea, if thou criest after knowledge, and liftest up thy
voice for understanding;

If thou seekest her as silver, and searchest for her as
for hid treasures;

Then shalt thou understand the fear of the LORD, and
find the knowledge of God.

For the LORD giveth wisdom: out of his mouth cometh
knowledge and understanding.

He layeth up sound wisdom for the righteous: he is a
buckler to them that walk uprightly.

Proverbs 2:1–7

The Lord thy God in the midst of thee is mighty; he will save, he will rejoice over thee with joy; he will rest in his love, he will joy over thee with singing.

Zephaniah 3:17

Get wisdom, get understanding: forget it not; neither decline from the words of my mouth.

Forsake her not, and she shall preserve thee: love her, and she shall keep thee.

Wisdom is the principal thing; therefore get wisdom: and with all thy getting get understanding.

Exalt her, and she shall promote thee: she shall bring thee to honour, when thou dost embrace her.

Proverbs 4:5–8

God's Eternal Gift

Verily, verily, I say unto you, He that heareth my word, and believeth on him that sent me, hath everlasting life, and shall not come into condemnation; but is passed from death unto life.

Verily, verily, I say unto you, the hour is coming, and now is, when the dead shall hear the voice of the Son of God: and they that hear shall live.

For as the Father hath life in himself; so hath he given to the Son to have life in himself.

John 5:24–26

And, behold, a certain lawyer stood up, and tempted him, saying, Master, what shall I do to inherit eternal life?

He said unto him, What is written in the law? how readest thou?

And he answering said, Thou shalt love the Lord thy God with all thy heart, and with all thy soul, and with all thy strength, and with all thy mind; and thy neighbour as thyself.

Luke 10:25–27

My sheep hear my voice, and I know them, and they follow me:

And I give unto them eternal life; and they shall never perish, neither shall any man pluck them out of my hand.

My Father, which gave them me, is greater than all; and no man is able to pluck them out of my Father's hand.

John 10:27–29

And no man hath ascended up to heaven, but he that came down from heaven, even the Son of man which is in heaven. . . .

That whosoever believeth in him should not perish, but have eternal life.

For God so loved the world, that he gave his only begotten Son, that whosoever believeth in him should not perish, but have everlasting life.

John 3:13, 15–16

This is a faithful saying, and worthy of all acceptation, that Christ Jesus came into the world to save sinners; of whom I am chief.

Howbeit for this cause I obtained mercy, that in me first Jesus Christ might shew forth all longsuffering, for a pattern to them which should hereafter believe on him to life everlasting.

Now unto the King eternal, immortal, invisible, the only wise God, be honour and glory for ever and ever. Amen.

1 Timothy 1:15–17

But thou, O man of God, flee these things; and follow after righteousness, godliness, faith, love, patience, meekness.

Fight the good fight of faith, lay hold on eternal life, whereunto thou art also called, and hast professed a good profession before many witnesses.

1 Timothy 6:11–12

But now being made free from sin, and become servants to God, ye have your fruit unto holiness, and the end everlasting life.

For the wages of sin is death; but the gift of God is eternal life through Jesus Christ our Lord.

Romans 6:22–23

Be not deceived; God is not mocked: for whatsoever a man soweth, that shall he also reap.

For he that soweth to his flesh shall of the flesh reap corruption; but he that soweth to the Spirit shall of the Spirit reap life everlasting.

Galatians 6:7–8

Jesus answered and said unto her, Whosoever drinketh of this water shall thirst again:

But whosoever drinketh of the water that I shall give him shall never thirst; but the water that I shall give him shall be in him a well of water springing up into everlasting life.

John 4:13–14

God's Holiness

Wherefore lift up the hands which hang down, and the feeble knees;

And make straight paths for your feet, lest that which is lame be turned out of the way; but let it rather be healed.

Follow peace with all men, and holiness, without which no man shall see the Lord.

Hebrews 12:12–14

Having therefore these promises, dearly beloved, let us cleanse ourselves from all filthiness of the flesh and spirit, perfecting holiness in the fear of God.

2 Corinthians 7:1

Give unto the Lord, ye kindreds of the people, give unto the Lord glory and strength.

Give unto the Lord the glory due unto his name: bring an offering, and come before him: worship the Lord in the beauty of holiness.

1 Chronicles 16:28–29

Then the eyes of the blind shall be opened, and the ears of the deaf shall be unstopped.

Then shall the lame man leap as an hart, and the tongue of the dumb sing: for in the wilderness shall waters break out, and streams in the desert.

And the parched ground shall become a pool, and the thirsty land springs of water: in the habitation of dragons, where each lay, shall be grass with reeds and rushes.

And an highway shall be there, and a way, and it shall be called The way of holiness; the unclean shall not pass over it; but it shall be for those: the wayfaring men, though fools, shall not err therein.

No lion shall be there, nor any ravenous beast shall go up thereon, it shall not be found there; but the redeemed shall walk there:

And the ransomed of the Lord shall return, and come to Zion with songs and everlasting joy upon their heads: they shall obtain joy and gladness, and sorrow and sighing shall flee away.

Isaiah 35:5–10

For God hath not called us unto uncleanness, but unto holiness.

He therefore that despiseth, despiseth not man, but God, who hath also given unto us his holy Spirit.

1 Thessalonians 4:7–8

PAUL, a servant of Jesus Christ, called to be an apostle, separated unto the gospel of God,

(Which he had promised afore by his prophets in the holy scriptures,)

Concerning his Son Jesus Christ our Lord, which was made of the seed of David according to the flesh;

And declared to be the Son of God with power, according to the spirit of holiness, by the resurrection from the dead:

By whom we have received grace and apostleship, for obedience to the faith among all nations, for his name:

Among whom are ye also the called of Jesus Christ.

Romans 1:1–6

Having therefore, brethren, boldness to enter into the holiest by the blood of Jesus,

By a new and living way, which he hath consecrated for us, through the veil, that is to say, his flesh;

And having an high priest over the house of God;

Let us draw near with a true heart in full assurance of faith, having our hearts sprinkled from an evil conscience, and our bodies washed with pure water.

Let us hold fast the profession of our faith without wavering; (for he is faithful that promised;)

And let us consider one another to provoke unto love and to good works.

Hebrews 10:19–24

Who is like unto thee, O Lord, among the gods? who is like thee, glorious in holiness, fearful in praises, doing wonders?

Thou stretchedst out thy right hand, the earth swallowed them.

Thou in thy mercy hast led forth the people which thou hast redeemed: thou hast guided them in thy strength unto thy holy habitation.

Exodus 15:11–13

And thou shalt put the mercy seat upon the ark of the testimony in the most holy place.

And thou shalt set the table without the vail, and the candlestick over against the table on the side of the tabernacle toward the south: and thou shalt put the table on the north side.

And thou shalt make an hanging for the door of the tent, of blue, and purple, and scarlet, and fine twined linen, wrought with needlework.

And thou shalt make for the hanging five pillars of shittim wood, and overlay them with gold, and their hooks shall be of gold: and thou shalt cast five sockets of brass for them.

Exodus 26:34–37

King James of 1769

y the mid-eighteenth century the wide variation in the various modernized printed texts of the Authorized Version, combined with the notorious accumulation of misprints, had reached the proportion of a scandal, and the Universities of Oxford and Cambridge both sought to produce an updated standard text. First of the two was the Cambridge edition of 1762, edited by F. S. Parris. This was effectively superseded by the 1769, edited by Benjamin Blayney, which became the Oxford standard text, and is reproduced almost unchanged in most current printings.

Parris and Blayney sought consistently to remove those elements of the 1611 and subsequent editions that they believed were due to the vagaries of printers, while incorporating most of the revised readings of the Cambridge editions of 1629 and 1638, and each also introducing a few improved readings of their own. They undertook the mammoth task of standardizing the wide variation in punctuation and spelling of the original, making many thousands of minor changes to the text; although some of these updates do alter the ostensible sense—as when the original text of Genesis 2:21 "in stead" ("in that place") was updated to read "instead" ("as an alternative").

In addition, Blayney and Parris thoroughly revised and greatly extended the italicization of "supplied" words not found in the original languages by cross-checking against the presumed source texts. Unfortunately, Blayney assumed that the translators of the 1611 New Testament had worked from the 1550 Stephanus edition of the *Textus Receptus*, rather than from the later editions of Beza; accordingly the current standard text mistakenly "corrects" around a dozen readings where Beza and Stephanus differ.

Like the 1611 edition, the 1769 Oxford edition included the Apocrypha, although Blayney consistently removed marginal cross-references to the Books of the Apocrypha wherever these had been provided by the original translators. Altogether, Blayney's 1769 text differed from the 1611 text in around 24,000 places. Since that date, only six further changes have been introduced to the standard text—although 30 of Blayney's proposed changes have subsequently been reverted. The Oxford University Press paperback edition of the Authorized King James Version provides the current standard text, and also includes the prefatory section "The Translators to the Reader."

For a period, Cambridge continued to issue Bibles using the Parris text, but the market demand for absolute standardization was now such that they eventually fell into line. Since the beginning of the nineteenth century, almost all printings of the Authorized Version have derived from the 1769 Oxford text—generally without Blayney's variant notes and cross references, and commonly excluding the Apocrypha.

From 1769, the text of the Authorized Version remained unchanged—and since, due to advances in printing technology, it could now be produced in very large editions for mass sale, it established complete dominance in public and ecclesiastical use in the Englishspeaking Protestant world.

God's Promises

He opened the rock, and the waters gushed out; they ran in the dry places like a river.

For he remembered his holy promise, and Abraham his servant.

And he brought forth his people with joy, and his chosen with gladness:

And gave them the lands of the heathen: and they inherited the labour of the people;

That they might observe his statutes, and keep his laws. Praise ye the LORD.

Psalm 105:41–45

For ye are all the children of God by faith in Christ Jesus.

For as many of you as have been baptized into Christ have put on Christ.

There is neither Jew nor Greek, there is neither bond nor free, there is neither male nor female: for ye are all one in Christ Jesus.

And if ye be Christ's, then are ye Abraham's seed, and heirs according to the promise.

Galatians 3:26–29

Therefore being by the right hand of God exalted, and having received of the Father the promise of the Holy Ghost, he hath shed forth this, which ye now see and hear.

For David is not ascended into the heavens: but he saith himself, The Lord said unto my Lord, Sit thou on my right hand,

Until I make thy foes thy footstool.

Therefore let all the house of Israel know assuredly, that God hath made that same Jesus, whom ye have crucified, both Lord and Christ. . . .

For the promise is unto you, and to your children, and to all that are afar off, even as many as the Lord our God shall call.

Acts 2:33–36, 39

For if they which are of the law be heirs, faith is made void, and the promise made of none effect:

Because the law worketh wrath: for where no law is, there is no transgression.

Therefore it is of faith, that it might be by grace; to the end the promise might be sure to all the seed; not to that only which is of the law, but to that also which is of the faith of Abraham; who is the father of us all, . . .

He staggered not at the promise of God through unbelief; but was strong in faith, giving glory to God;

And being fully persuaded that, what he had promised, he was able also to perform.

And therefore it was imputed to him for righteousness.

Romans 4:14–16, 20–22

And said unto them, Thus it is written, and thus it behoved Christ to suffer, and to rise from the dead the third day:

And that repentance and remission of sins should be preached in his name among all nations, beginning at Jerusalem.

And ye are witnesses of these things.

And, behold, I send the promise of my Father upon you: but tarry ye in the city of Jerusalem, until ye be endued with power from on high.

Luke 24:46–49

For when God made promise to Abraham, because he could swear by no greater, he sware by himself,

Saying, Surely blessing I will bless thee, and multiplying I will multiply thee.

And so, after he had patiently endured, he obtained the promise. . . .

Wherein God, willing more abundantly to shew unto the heirs of promise the immutability of his counsel, confirmed it by an oath:

That by two immutable things, in which it was impossible for God to lie, we might have a strong consolation, who have fled for refuge to lay hold upon the hope set before us.

Hebrews 6:13–15, 17–18

If thou put the brethren in remembrance of these things, thou shalt be a good minister of Jesus Christ, nourished up in the words of faith and of good doctrine, whereunto thou hast attained.

But refuse profane and old wives' fables, and exercise thyself rather unto godliness.

For bodily exercise profiteth little: but godliness is profitable unto all things, having promise of the life that now is, and of that which is to come.

1 Timothy 4:6–8

The Lord is not slack concerning his promise, as some men count slackness; but is longsuffering to us-ward, not willing that any should perish, but that all should come to repentance. . . .

Nevertheless we, according to his promise, look for new heavens and a new earth, wherein dwelleth righteousness.

Wherefore, beloved, seeing that ye look for such things, be diligent that ye may be found of him in peace, without spot, and blameless.

2 Peter 3:9, 13–14

God's Covenant

Who also hath made us able ministers of the new testament; not of the letter, but of the spirit: for the letter killeth, but the spirit giveth life.

2 Corinthians 3:6

Now therefore, if ye will obey my voice indeed, and keep my covenant, then ye shall be a peculiar treasure unto me above all people: for all the earth is mine:

And ye shall be unto me a kingdom of priests, and an holy nation. These are the words which thou shalt speak unto the children of Israel.

And Moses came and called for the elders of the people, and laid before their faces all these words which the Lord commanded him.

And all the people answered together, and said, All that the Lord hath spoken we will do. And Moses returned the words of the people unto the Lord.

Exodus 19:5–8

And it came to pass, that, when the sun went down, and it was dark, behold a smoking furnace, and a burning lamp that passed between those pieces.

In the same day the LORD made a covenant with Abram, saying, Unto thy seed have I given this land, from the river of Egypt unto the great river, the river Euphrates:

The Kenites, and the Kenizzites, and the Kadmonites,

And the Hittites, and the Perizzites, and the Rephaims,

And the Amorites, and the Canaanites, and the Girgashites, and the Jebusites.

Genesis 15:17–21

And to Jesus the mediator of the new covenant, and to the blood of sprinkling, that speaketh better things than that of Abel.

See that ye refuse not him that speaketh. For if they escaped not who refused him that spake on earth, much more shall not we escape, if we turn away from him that speaketh from heaven:

Whose voice then shook the earth: but now he hath promised, saying, Yet once more I shake not the earth only, but also heaven.

And this word, Yet once more, signifieth the removing of those things that are shaken, as of things that are made, that those things which cannot be shaken may remain.

Wherefore we receiving a kingdom which cannot be moved, let us have grace, whereby we may serve God acceptably with reverence and godly fear.

Hebrews 12:24–28

BEHOLD, I will send my messenger, and he shall prepare the way before me: and the Lord, whom ye seek, shall suddenly come to his temple, even the messenger of the covenant, whom ye delight in: behold, he shall come, saith the Lord of hosts.

But who may abide the day of his coming? and who shall stand when he appeareth? for he is like a refiner's fire, and like fullers' soap:

And he shall sit as a refiner and purifier of silver: and he shall purify the sons of Levi, and purge them as gold and silver, that they may offer unto the Lord an offering in righteousness.

Malachi 3:1–3

But now hath he obtained a more excellent ministry, by how much also he is the mediator of a better covenant, which was established upon better promises.

For if that first covenant had been faultless, then should no place have been sought for the second.

For finding fault with them, he saith, Behold, the days come, saith the Lord, when I will make a new covenant with the house of Israel and with the house of Judah:

Not according to the covenant that I made with their fathers in the day when I took them by the hand to lead them out of the land of Egypt; because they continued not in my covenant, and I regarded them not, saith the Lord.

For this is the covenant that I will make with the house of Israel after those days, saith the Lord; I will put my laws into their mind, and write them in their hearts: and I will be to them a God, and they shall be to me a people.

Hebrews 8:6–10

But this shall be the covenant that I will make with the house of Israel; after those days, saith the Lord, I will put my law in their inward parts, and write it in their hearts; and will be their God, and they shall be my people.

Jeremiah 31:33

Now the God of peace, that brought again from the dead our Lord Jesus, that great shepherd of the sheep, through the blood of the everlasting covenant,

Make you perfect in every good work to do his will, working in you that which is wellpleasing in his sight, through Jesus Christ; to whom be glory for ever and ever. Amen.

Hebrews 13:20–21

And as they were eating, Jesus took bread, and blessed it, and brake it, and gave it to the disciples, and said, Take, eat; this is my body.

And he took the cup, and gave thanks, and gave it to them, saying, Drink ye all of it;

For this is my blood of the new testament, which is shed for many for the remission of sins.

But I say unto you, I will not drink henceforth of this fruit of the vine, until that day when I drink it new with you in my Father's kingdom.

And when they had sung an hymn, they went out into the mount of Olives.

Matthew 26:26–30

God's Goodness

Yea, though I walk through the valley of the shadow of death, I will fear no evil: for thou art with me; thy rod and thy staff they comfort me.

Thou preparest a table before me in the presence of mine enemies: thou anointest my head with oil; my cup runneth over.

Surely goodness and mercy shall follow me all the days of my life: and I will dwell in the house of the LORD for ever.

Psalm 23:4–6

Teach me thy way, O LORD, and lead me in a plain path, because of mine enemies.

Deliver me not over unto the will of mine enemies: for false witnesses are risen up against me, and such as breathe out cruelty.

I had fainted, unless I had believed to see the goodness of the LORD in the land of the living.

Wait on the LORD: be of good courage, and he shall strengthen thine heart: wait, I say, on the LORD.

Psalm 27:11–14

Oh how great is thy goodness, which thou hast laid up for them that fear thee; which thou hast wrought for them that trust in thee before the sons of men!

Thou shalt hide them in the secret of thy presence from the pride of man: thou shalt keep them secretly in a pavilion from the strife of tongues.

Blessed be the LORD: for he hath shewed me his marvellous kindness in a strong city.

Psalm 31:19–21

But we are sure that the judgment of God is according to truth against them which commit such things.

And thinkest thou this, O man, that judgest them which do such things, and doest the same, that thou shalt escape the judgment of God?

Or despisest thou the riches of his goodness and forbearance and longsuffering; not knowing that the goodness of God leadeth thee to repentance?

Romans 2:2–4

And the LORD descended in the cloud, and stood with him there, and proclaimed the name of the LORD.

And the LORD passed by before him, and proclaimed, The LORD, The LORD God, merciful and gracious, longsuffering, and abundant in goodness and truth.

Exodus 34:5–6

Why boastest thou thyself in mischief, O mighty man? the goodness of God endureth continually.

Psalm 52:1

Boast not against the branches. But if thou boast, thou bearest not the root, but the root thee.

Thou wilt say then, The branches were broken off, that I might be graffed in.

Well; because of unbelief they were broken off, and thou standest by faith. Be not highminded, but fear:

For if God spared not the natural branches, take heed lest he also spare not thee.

Behold therefore the goodness and severity of God: on them which fell, severity; but toward thee, goodness, if thou continue in his goodness: otherwise thou also shalt be cut off.

And they also, if they abide not still in unbelief, shall be graffed in: for God is able to graff them in again.

Romans 11:18–23

But the fruit of the Spirit is love, joy, peace, longsuffering, gentleness, goodness, faith.

Galatians 5:22

God's Favor

So shalt thou find favour and good understanding in the sight of God and man.

Proverbs 3:4

Blessed is the man that heareth me, watching daily at my gates, waiting at the posts of my doors.

For whoso findeth me findeth life, and shall obtain favour of the Lord.

Proverbs 8:34–35

The law of the wise is a fountain of life, to depart from the snares of death.

Good understanding giveth favour: but the way of transgressors is hard.

Proverbs 13:14–15

The king's wrath is as the roaring of a lion; but his favour is as dew upon the grass.

Proverbs 19:12

The wrath of a king is as messengers of death: but a wise man will pacify it.

In the light of the king's countenance is life; and his favour is as a cloud of the latter rain.

How much better is it to get wisdom than gold! and to get understanding rather to be chosen than silver!

Proverbs 16:14–16

Sing unto the Lord, O ye saints of his, and give thanks at the remembrance of his holiness.

For his anger endureth but a moment; in his favour is life: weeping may endure for a night, but joy cometh in the morning.

Psalm 30:4–5

But let all those that put their trust in thee rejoice: let them ever shout for joy, because thou defendest them: let them also that love thy name be joyful in thee.

For thou, Lord, wilt bless the righteous; with favour wilt thou compass him as with a shield.

Psalm 5:11–12

And the angel said unto her, Fear not, Mary: for thou hast found favour with God.

And, behold, thou shalt conceive in thy womb, and bring forth a son, and shalt call his name JESUS.

Luke 1:30–31

Remember me, O Lord, with the favour that thou
bearest unto thy people: O visit me with thy salvation;
That I may see the good of thy chosen, that I may
rejoice in the gladness of thy nation, that I may glory
with thine inheritance.

Psalm 106:4–5

Let them shout for joy, and be glad, that favour my
righteous cause: yea, let them say continually, Let the
Lord be magnified, which hath pleasure in the prosperity
of his servant.

And my tongue shall speak of thy righteousness and
of thy praise all the day long.

Psalm 35:27–28

God's Heaven

The Lord is in his holy temple, the Lord's throne is in heaven: his eyes behold, his eyelids try, the children of men.

Psalm 11:4

Behold, I give unto you power to tread on serpents and scorpions, and over all the power of the enemy: and nothing shall by any means hurt you.

Notwithstanding in this rejoice not, that the spirits are subject unto you; but rather rejoice, because your names are written in heaven.

In that hour Jesus rejoiced in spirit, and said, I thank thee, O Father, Lord of heaven and earth, that thou hast hid these things from the wise and prudent, and hast revealed them unto babes: even so, Father; for so it seemed good in thy sight.

Luke 10:19–21

I say unto you, that likewise joy shall be in heaven over one sinner that repenteth, more than over ninety and nine just persons, which need no repentance.

Luke 15:7

Since we heard of your faith in Christ Jesus, and of the love which ye have to all the saints,

For the hope which is laid up for you in heaven, whereof ye heard before in the word of the truth of the gospel;

Which is come unto you, as it is in all the world; and bringeth forth fruit, as it doth also in you, since the day ye heard of it, and knew the grace of God in truth.

Colossians 1:4–6

And he saith unto him, Verily, verily, I say unto you, Hereafter ye shall see heaven open, and the angels of God ascending and descending upon the Son of man.

John 1:51

I will lift up mine eyes unto the hills, from whence cometh my help.

My help cometh from the Lord, which made heaven and earth.

He will not suffer thy foot to be moved: he that keepeth thee will not slumber.

Psalm 121:1–3

THUS SAITH the Lord, The heaven is my throne, and the earth is my footstool: where is the house that ye build unto me? and where is the place of my rest?

For all those things hath mine hand made, and all those things have been, saith the Lord: but to this man will I look, even to him that is poor and of a contrite spirit, and trembleth at my word.

Isaiah 66:1–2

AND I saw a new heaven and a new earth: for the first heaven and the first earth were passed away; and there was no more sea.

And I John saw the holy city, new Jerusalem, coming down from God out of heaven, prepared as a bride adorned for her husband.

And I heard a great voice out of heaven saying, Behold, the tabernacle of God is with men, and he will dwell with them, and they shall be his people, and God himself shall be with them, and be their God.

And God shall wipe away all tears from their eyes; and there shall be no more death, neither sorrow, nor crying, neither shall there be any more pain: for the former things are passed away.

Revelation 21:1–4

Then Jesus said unto them, Verily, verily, I say unto you, Moses gave you not that bread from heaven; but my Father giveth you the true bread from heaven.

For the bread of God is he which cometh down from heaven, and giveth life unto the world.

Then said they unto him, Lord, evermore give us this bread.

And Jesus said unto them, I am the bread of life: he that cometh to me shall never hunger; and he that believeth on me shall never thirst.

But I said unto you, That ye also have seen me, and believe not.

All that the Father giveth me shall come to me; and him that cometh to me I will in no wise cast out.

For I came down from heaven, not to do mine own will, but the will of him that sent me.

And this is the Father's will which hath sent me, that of all which he hath given me I should lose nothing, but should raise it up again at the last day.

John 6:32–39

The Profound Influence of the King James Version

The beauty of the King James Version, as well as its enormous influence, can never be exaggerated. The new version won wide acceptance among the people of the Englishspeaking world and easily eclipsed all previous versions of the Bible. Nonsectarian in tone and approach, it did not favor one shade of theological or ecclesiastical opinion over another. With the translators' feeling for prose rhythm, never was a version of the Bible more admirably suited for reading aloud in public. It proved so acceptable that it remained for three centuries, without a serious rival version, the Bible of Englishspeaking Protestants. To this day, the King James Version remains deeply revered.

The precision of translation for which it is historically renowned, the simple yet grand language, and its majesty of style enabled this version of the Word of God to become the mainspring of the religion, language, and legal foundations of English civilization. It has inspired virtually every great English writer since the seventeenth century—from John Dryden to

Herman Melville to Henry Wadsworth Longfellow to the Rev. Martin Luther King Jr. "Without the King James Bible," Alister McGrath stated, "there would have been no *Paradise Lost*, no *Pilgrim's Progress*, no Handel's *Messiah*, no Negro spirituals, and no Gettysburg Address." These, and innumerable other works, were inspired by the language of this Bible. That the culture of the Englishspeaking world would have been immeasurably diminished without this Bible is certain.

John Bunyan's
Pilgrim's Progress

God's Angels

The angel of the LORD encampeth round about them that fear him, and delivereth them.

O taste and see that the LORD is good: blessed is the man that trusteth in him.

O fear the LORD, ye his saints: for there is no want to them that fear him.

The young lions do lack, and suffer hunger: but they that seek the LORD shall not want any good thing.

Psalm 34:7–10

Jesus answered and said unto them, Ye do err, not knowing the scriptures, nor the power of God.

For in the resurrection they neither marry, nor are given in marriage, but are as the angels of God in heaven.

But as touching the resurrection of the dead, have ye not read that which was spoken unto you by God, saying,

I am the God of Abraham, and the God of Isaac, and the God of Jacob? God is not the God of the dead, but of the living.

Matthew 22:29–32

And, behold, there was a great earthquake: for the angel of the Lord descended from heaven, and came and rolled back the stone from the door, and sat upon it.

His countenance was like lightning, and his raiment white as snow:

And for fear of him the keepers did shake, and became as dead men.

And the angel answered and said unto the women, Fear not ye: for I know that ye seek Jesus, which was crucified.

He is not here: for he is risen, as he said. Come, see the place where the Lord lay.

And go quickly, and tell his disciples that he is risen from the dead; and, behold, he goeth before you into Galilee; there shall ye see him: lo, I have told you.

Matthew 28:2–7

And I saw a strong angel proclaiming with a loud voice, Who is worthy to open the book, and to loose the seals thereof?

And no man in heaven, nor in earth, neither under the earth, was able to open the book, neither to look thereon.

And I wept much, because no man was found worthy to open and to read the book, neither to look thereon.

And one of the elders saith unto me, Weep not: behold, the Lion of the tribe of Juda, the Root of David, hath prevailed to open the book, and to loose the seven seals thereof.

Revelation 5:2–5

Praise ye him, all his angels: praise ye him, all his hosts.

Praise ye him, sun and moon: praise him, all ye stars of light.

Praise him, ye heavens of heavens, and ye waters that be above the heavens.

Let them praise the name of the LORD: for he commanded, and they were created.

He hath also stablished them for ever and ever: he hath made a decree which shall not pass.

Psalm 148:2–6

And the angel of the LORD called unto him out of heaven, and said, Abraham, Abraham: and he said, Here am I.

And he said, Lay not thine hand upon the lad, neither do thou any thing unto him: for now I know that thou fearest God, seeing thou hast not withheld thy son, thine only son from me.

And Abraham lifted up his eyes, and looked, and behold behind him a ram caught in a thicket by his horns: and Abraham went and took the ram, and offered him up for a burnt offering in the stead of his son.

And Abraham called the name of that place Jehovahjireh: as it is said to this day, In the mount of the LORD it shall be seen.

Genesis 22:11–14

There shall no evil befall thee, neither shall any plague come nigh thy dwelling.

For he shall give his angels charge over thee, to keep thee in all thy ways.

They shall bear thee up in their hands, lest thou dash thy foot against a stone.

Psalm 91:10–12

And the angel of the Lord called unto Abraham out of heaven the second time,

And said, By myself have I sworn, saith the Lord, for because thou hast done this thing, and hast not withheld thy son, thine only son:

That in blessing I will bless thee, and in multiplying I will multiply thy seed as the stars of the heaven, and as the sand which is upon the sea shore; and thy seed shall possess the gate of his enemies;

And in thy seed shall all the nations of the earth be blessed; because thou hast obeyed my voice.

So Abraham returned unto his young men, and they rose up and went together to Beersheba; and Abraham dwelt at Beersheba.

Genesis 22:15–19

Our Salvation

That if thou shalt confess with thy mouth the Lord Jesus, and shalt believe in thine heart that God hath raised him from the dead, thou shalt be saved.

For with the heart man believeth unto righteousness; and with the mouth confession is made unto salvation.

For the scripture saith, Whosoever believeth on him shall not be ashamed.

For there is no difference between the Jew and the Greek: for the same Lord over all is rich unto all that call upon him.

For whosoever shall call upon the name of the Lord shall be saved.

Romans 10:9–13

Not by works of righteousness which we have done, but according to his mercy he saved us, by the washing of regeneration, and renewing of the Holy Ghost;

Which he shed on us abundantly through Jesus Christ our Saviour.

Titus 3:5–6

For by grace are ye saved through faith; and that not of yourselves: it is the gift of God:

Not of works, lest any man should boast.

For we are his workmanship, created in Christ Jesus unto good works, which God hath before ordained that we should walk in them.

Ephesians 2:8–10

For God so loved the world, that he gave his only begotten Son, that whosoever believeth in him should not perish, but have everlasting life.

For God sent not his Son into the world to condemn the world; but that the world through him might be saved.

John 3:16–17

Wherefore, my beloved, as ye have always obeyed, not as in my presence only, but now much more in my absence, work out your own salvation with fear and trembling.

For it is God which worketh in you both to will and to do of his good pleasure.

Philippians 2:12–13

Lead me in thy truth, and teach me: for thou art the God of my salvation; on thee do I wait all the day.

Psalm 25:5

The Lord is my light and my salvation; whom shall I fear? The Lord is the strength of my life; of whom shall I be afraid?

Psalm 27:1

But we are bound to give thanks always to God for you, brethren beloved of the Lord, because God hath from the beginning chosen you to salvation through sanctification of the Spirit and belief of the truth:

Whereunto he called you by our gospel, to the obtaining of the glory of our Lord Jesus Christ.

2 Thessalonians 2:13–14

Our Reward

If thine enemy be hungry, give him bread to eat; and if he be thirsty, give him water to drink:

For thou shalt heap coals of fire upon his head, and the Lord shall reward thee.

Proverbs 25:21–22

The wicked worketh a deceitful work: but to him that soweth righteousness shall be a sure reward.

As righteousness tendeth to life: so he that pursueth evil pursueth it to his own death.

Proverbs 11:18–19

So I was great, and increased more than all that were before me in Jerusalem: also my wisdom remained with me.

And whatsoever mine eyes desired I kept not from them, I withheld not my heart from any joy; for my heart rejoiced in all my labour: and this was my portion of all my labour.

Ecclesiastes 2:9–10

Behold, the Lord GOD will come with strong hand, and his arm shall rule for him: behold, his reward is with him, and his work before him.

He shall feed his flock like a shepherd: he shall gather the lambs with his arm, and carry them in his bosom, and shall gently lead those that are with young.

Isaiah 40:10–11

The fear of the LORD is clean, enduring for ever: the judgments of the LORD are true and righteous altogether.

More to be desired are they than gold, yea, than much fine gold: sweeter also than honey and the honeycomb.

Moreover by them is thy servant warned: and in keeping of them there is great reward.

Psalm 19:9–11

Now he that planteth and he that watereth are one: and every man shall receive his own reward according to his own labour.

For we are labourers together with God: ye are God's husbandry, ye are God's building. According to the grace of God which is given unto me, as a wise masterbuilder, I have laid the foundation, and another buildeth thereon. But let every man take heed how he buildeth thereupon.

1 Corinthians 3:8–10

Look to yourselves, that we lose not those things which we have wrought, but that we receive a full reward.

Whosoever transgresseth, and abideth not in the doctrine of Christ, hath not God. He that abideth in the doctrine of Christ, he hath both the Father and the Son.

2 John 8–9

But love ye your enemies, and do good, and lend, hoping for nothing again; and your reward shall be great, and ye shall be the children of the Highest: for he is kind unto the unthankful and to the evil.

Be ye therefore merciful, as your Father also is merciful.

Luke 6:35–36

Let no man beguile you of your reward in a voluntary humility and worshipping of angels, intruding into those things which he hath not seen, vainly puffed up by his fleshly mind,

And not holding the Head, from which all the body by joints and bands having nourishment ministered, and knit together, increaseth with the increase of God.

Colossians 2:18–19

Our Encouragement

Who is this King of glory? The LORD strong and mighty, the LORD mighty in battle.

Lift up your heads, O ye gates; even lift them up, ye everlasting doors; and the King of glory shall come in.

Psalm 24:8–9

Because thy lovingkindness is better than life, my lips shall praise thee.

Thus will I bless thee while I live: I will lift up my hands in thy name.

My soul shall be satisfied as with marrow and fatness; and my mouth shall praise thee with joyful lips.

Psalm 63:3–5

For I am not ashamed of the gospel of Christ: for it is the power of God unto salvation to every one that believeth; to the Jew first, and also to the Greek.

For therein is the righteousness of God revealed from faith to faith: as it is written, The just shall live by faith.

Romans 1:16–17

The LORD is thy keeper: the LORD is thy shade upon thy right hand.

The sun shall not smite thee by day, nor the moon by night. . . .

The LORD shall preserve thy going out and thy coming in from this time forth, and even for evermore.

Psalm 121:5–6, 8

Humble yourselves in the sight of the Lord, and he shall lift you up.

Speak not evil one of another, brethren. He that speaketh evil of his brother, and judgeth his brother, speaketh evil of the law, and judgeth the law: but if thou judge the law, thou art not a doer of the law, but a judge.

James 4:10–11

If any thing be revealed to another that sitteth by, let the first hold his peace.

For ye may all prophesy one by one, that all may learn, and all may be comforted.

And the spirits of the prophets are subject to the prophets.

For God is not the author of confusion, but of peace, as in all churches of the saints.

1 *Corinthians* 14:30–33

FOR I would that ye knew what great conflict I have for you, and for them at Laodicea, and for as many as have not seen my face in the flesh;

That their hearts might be comforted, being knit together in love, and unto all riches of the full assurance of understanding, to the acknowledgement of the mystery of God, and of the Father, and of Christ;

In whom are hid all the treasures of wisdom and knowledge.

Colossians 2:1–3

Our Joy

If ye keep my commandments, ye shall abide in my love; even as I have kept my Father's commandments, and abide in his love.

These things have I spoken unto you, that my joy might remain in you, and that your joy might be full.

John 15:10–11

Rejoice in the Lord alway: and again I say, Rejoice.

Let your moderation be known unto all men. The Lord is at hand.

Philippians 4:4–5

Yet I will rejoice in the LORD, I will joy in the God of my salvation.

The LORD God is my strength, and he will make my feet like hinds' feet, and he will make me to walk upon mine high places.

Habakkuk 3:18–19

Wherein ye greatly rejoice, though now for a season, if need be, ye are in heaviness through manifold temptations:

That the trial of your faith, being much more precious than of gold that perisheth, though it be tried with fire, might be found unto praise and honour and glory at the appearing of Jesus Christ:

Whom having not seen, ye love; in whom, though now ye see him not, yet believing, ye rejoice with joy unspeakable and full of glory:

Receiving the end of your faith, even the salvation of your souls.

1 Peter 1:6–9

I have set the Lord always before me: because he is at my right hand, I shall not be moved.

Therefore my heart is glad, and my glory rejoiceth: my flesh also shall rest in hope.

For thou wilt not leave my soul in hell; neither wilt thou suffer thine Holy One to see corruption.

Thou wilt shew me the path of life: in thy presence is fulness of joy; at thy right hand there are pleasures for evermore.

Psalm 16:8–11

My brethren, count it all joy when ye fall into divers temptations;

Knowing this, that the trying of your faith worketh patience.

James 1:2–3

For I rejoiced greatly, when the brethren came and testified of the truth that is in thee, even as thou walkest in the truth.

I have no greater joy than to hear that my children walk in truth.

3 John 3–4

His lord said unto him, Well done, thou good and faithful servant: thou hast been faithful over a few things, I will make thee ruler over many things: enter thou into the joy of thy lord.

Matthew 25:21

The King James Bible in Everyday Life

For the first time, England was reading one Bible at home and hearing the same Bible at church. Albert S. Cook said, "It thus became bound up with the life of the nation. Since it stilled all controversy over the best rendering, it gradually came to be accepted as so far absolute in the minds of myriads, there was no distinction between this version and the original texts, and they may almost be said to have believed in the literal inspiration of the very words that composed it."

Yet the importance of the Bible transcended that of personal religious devotion and faith. It became central to the life of English society in a way that we cannot begin to imagine today. Many families could afford only one book—a Bible—and for many years this was the only English translation of the Bible available. Generations of young people learned to read from the words they found in the King James Version. Many memorized biblical passages and found that their written and spoken English was shaped by the language and imagery of this Bible. For most readers, it was regarded as their social, economic, political, and spiritual text.

The great Winston Churchill also noted that the scholars who produced the King James Version had forged an enduring link, literary and religious, between the Englishspeaking people spread across the world. This translation naturally became a part of their everyday life for many generations. Andrew Motion, Poet Laureate of the United Kingdom from 1999 to 2009, said of it: "To read it is to feel simultaneously at home, a citizen of the world, and a traveler through eternity."

David Crystal, a linguistic expert on the development of the English language, adds that the King James Version "did something that nobody else had done, or nothing else had done in the history of the language previously. Not even Shakespeare had managed to do as much . . . no other text in the history of the English language has done as much as the Bible to shape our modern idiom." Hundreds of idioms or figures of speech—semiproverbial or proverbial expressions that might have come from everyday usage but had never been made prominent in literature—became prominent through this Bible.

C. S. Lewis said that whenever we use words such as "beautiful," "longsuffering," "peacemaker," or "scapegoat," it is due to the influence of the King James Version. However, it is not only in the words or the many phrases in our language that the force and influence of the King James Version is felt, but in the very rhythm of our language—the very way that we breathe and pause and rise and fall as we speak. Beyond that, David Simpson, a member of the British Parliament, said regarding the 400th anniversary of this translation, "It is not only our literature and language that has been influenced by the King James Version. It has had an extraordinary and beneficial influence upon political and constitutional affairs. It was the Bible of Milton and of the Protectorate; later, it was the Bible of the Glorious Revolution, which gave us a constitutional monarchy and parliamentary democracy. It was the Bible of Whitefield and the Wesleys that saved this realm from the brutality and blood of the French Revolution. It was the Bible carried by the founding fathers of the United States that helped to forge that land and give the world that great democratic powerhouse."

While men and women have celebrated the manifold influence of the King James Version for 400 years, Steven Houck reminds us that "even more important, we must recognize that the King James Version is the Word of God that He has graciously and lovingly given to His Englishspeaking Church. It is a faithful translation of the inspired originals that have been providentially preserved by God in the thousands of manuscripts that have come down to us. Thus we can be assured that with the King James Version of the Bible we have the authoritative Word of God."

Our Praise and Worship

And they rose early in the morning, and went forth into the wilderness of Tekoa: and as they went forth, Jehoshaphat stood and said, Hear me, O Judah, and ye inhabitants of Jerusalem; believe in the Lord your God, so shall ye be established; believe his prophets, so shall ye prosper.

And when he had consulted with the people, he appointed singers unto the Lord, and that should praise the beauty of holiness, as they went out before the army, and to say, Praise the Lord; for his mercy endureth for ever.

2 Chronicles 20:20–21

While I live will I praise the Lord: I will sing praises unto my God while I have any being.

Put not your trust in princes, nor in the son of man, in whom there is no help.

Psalm 146:2–3

115

Let them praise the name of the LORD: for he commanded, and they were created.

He hath also stablished them for ever and ever: he hath made a decree which shall not pass.

Psalm 148:5–6

Praise ye the LORD. Praise God in his sanctuary: praise him in the firmament of his power.

Praise him for his mighty acts: praise him according to his excellent greatness. . . .

Let every thing that hath breath praise the LORD. Praise ye the LORD.

Psalm 150:1–2, 6

I will praise thee, O LORD, with my whole heart; I will shew forth all thy marvellous works.

I will be glad and rejoice in thee: I will sing praise to thy name, O thou most High.

Psalm 9:1–2

I will bless the LORD at all times: his praise shall continually be in my mouth.

My soul shall make her boast in the LORD: the humble shall hear thereof, and be glad.

O magnify the LORD with me, and let us exalt his name together.

Psalm 34:1–3

The meek shall eat and be satisfied: they shall praise the LORD that seek him: your heart shall live for ever.

All the ends of the world shall remember and turn unto the LORD: and all the kindreds of the nations shall worship before thee.

Psalm 22:26–27

I will sing unto the LORD as long as I live: I will sing praise to my God while I have my being.

My meditation of him shall be sweet: I will be glad in the LORD.

Let the sinners be consumed out of the earth, and let the wicked be no more. Bless thou the LORD, O my soul. Praise ye the LORD.

Psalm 104:33–35

For the LORD is a great God, and a great King above all gods.

In his hand are the deep places of the earth: the strength of the hills is his also.

The sea is his, and he made it: and his hands formed the dry land.

O come, let us worship and bow down: let us kneel before the LORD our maker.

Psalm 95:3–6

Our Courage

Be strong and of a good courage: for unto this people shalt thou divide for an inheritance the land, which I sware unto their fathers to give them.

Only be thou strong and very courageous, that thou mayest observe to do according to all the law, which Moses my servant commanded thee: turn not from it to the right hand or to the left, that thou mayest prosper whithersoever thou goest.

This book of the law shall not depart out of thy mouth; but thou shalt meditate therein day and night, that thou mayest observe to do according to all that is written therein: for then thou shalt make thy way prosperous, and then thou shalt have good success.

Joshua 1:6–8

Wait on the LORD: be of good courage, and he shall strengthen thine heart: wait, I say, on the LORD.

Psalm 27:14

Arise; for this matter belongeth unto thee: we also will be with thee: be of good courage, and do it.

Then arose Ezra, and made the chief priests, the Levites, and all Israel, to swear that they should do according to this word. And they sware.

Ezra 10:4–5

Be strong and of a good courage, fear not, nor be afraid of them: for the LORD thy God, he it is that doth go with thee; he will not fail thee, nor forsake thee.

And Moses called unto Joshua, and said unto him in the sight of all Israel, Be strong and of a good courage: for thou must go with this people unto the land which the LORD hath sworn unto their fathers to give them; and thou shalt cause them to inherit it.

Deuteronomy 31:6–7

Be strong and courageous, be not afraid nor dismayed for the king of Assyria, nor for all the multitude that is with him: for there be more with us than with him: with him is an arm of flesh; but with us is the LORD our God to help us, and to fight our battles.

And the people rested themselves upon the words of Hezekiah king of Judah.

2 Chronicles 32:7–8

And when Asa heard these words, and the prophecy of Oded the prophet, he took courage, and put away the abominable idols out of all the land of Judah and Benjamin, and out of the cities which he had taken from mount Ephraim, and renewed the altar of the LORD, that was before the porch of the LORD.

And he gathered all Judah and Benjamin, and the strangers with them out of Ephraim and Manasseh, and out of Simeon: for they fell to him out of Israel in abundance, when they saw that the LORD his God was with him.

2 Chronicles 15:8–9

As the Father knoweth me, even so know I the Father: and I lay down my life for the sheep.

And other sheep I have, which are not of this fold: them also I must bring, and they shall hear my voice; and there shall be one fold, and one shepherd.

Therefore doth my Father love me, because I lay down my life, that I might take it again.

No man taketh it from me, but I lay it down of myself. I have power to lay it down, and I have power to take it again. This commandment have I received of my Father.

John 10:15–18

Then cometh Jesus with them unto a place called Gethsemane, and saith unto the disciples, Sit ye here, while I go and pray yonder.

And he took with him Peter and the two sons of Zebedee, and began to be sorrowful and very heavy.

Then saith he unto them, My soul is exceeding sorrowful, even unto death: tarry ye here, and watch with me.

And he went a little farther, and fell on his face, and prayed, saying, O my Father, if it be possible, let this cup pass from me: nevertheless not as I will, but as thou wilt.

Matthew 26:36–39

Our Heart

Search me, O God, and know my heart: try me, and know my thoughts:

And see if there be any wicked way in me, and lead me in the way everlasting.

Psalm 139:23–24

But the Lord said unto Samuel, Look not on his countenance, or on the height of his stature; because I have refused him: for the Lord seeth not as man seeth; for man looketh on the outward appearance, but the Lord looketh on the heart.

1 Samuel 16:7

With my whole heart have I sought thee: O let me not wander from thy commandments.

Thy word have I hid in mine heart, that I might not sin against thee.

Blessed art thou, O Lord: teach me thy statutes.

Psalm 119:10–12

Praise ye the Lord. I will praise the Lord with my whole heart, in the assembly of the upright, and in the congregation.

The works of the Lord are great, sought out of all them that have pleasure therein.

His work is honourable and glorious: and his righteousness endureth for ever.

He hath made his wonderful works to be remembered: the Lord is gracious and full of compassion.

Psalm 111:1–4

Light is sown for the righteous, and gladness for the upright in heart.

Rejoice in the LORD, ye righteous; and give thanks at the remembrance of his holiness.

Psalm 97:11–12

For I will set mine eyes upon them for good, and I will bring them again to this land: and I will build them, and not pull them down; and I will plant them, and not pluck them up.

And I will give them an heart to know me, that I am the Lord: and they shall be my people, and I will be their God: for they shall return unto me with their whole heart.

Jeremiah 24:6–7

Trust in the Lord with all thine heart; and lean not unto thine own understanding.

In all thy ways acknowledge him, and he shall direct thy paths.

Proverbs 3:5–6

For I know the thoughts that I think toward you, saith the Lord, thoughts of peace, and not of evil, to give you an expected end.

Then shall ye call upon me, and ye shall go and pray unto me, and I will hearken unto you.

And ye shall seek me, and find me, when ye shall search for me with all your heart.

Jeremiah 29:11–13

That if thou shalt confess with thy mouth the Lord Jesus, and shalt believe in thine heart that God hath raised him from the dead, thou shalt be saved.

For with the heart man believeth unto righteousness; and with the mouth confession is made unto salvation.

Romans 10:9–10

Our Inheritance

The LORD is the portion of mine inheritance and of my cup: thou maintainest my lot.

The lines are fallen unto me in pleasant places; yea, I have a goodly heritage.

I will bless the LORD, who hath given me counsel: my reins also instruct me in the night seasons.

Psalm 16:5–7

The LORD knoweth the days of the upright: and their inheritance shall be for ever.

They shall not be ashamed in the evil time: and in the days of famine they shall be satisfied.

Psalm 37:18–19

And this I say, that the covenant, that was confirmed before of God in Christ, the law, which was four hundred and thirty years after, cannot disannul, that it should make the promise of none effect.

For if the inheritance be of the law, it is no more of promise: but God gave it to Abraham by promise.

Galatians 3:17–18

O clap your hands, all ye people; shout unto God with the voice of triumph.

For the Lord most high is terrible; he is a great King over all the earth.

He shall subdue the people under us, and the nations under our feet.

He shall choose our inheritance for us, the excellency of Jacob whom he loved.

Psalm 47:1–4

Giving thanks unto the Father, which hath made us meet to be partakers of the inheritance of the saints in light:

Who hath delivered us from the power of darkness, and hath translated us into the kingdom of his dear Son:

In whom we have redemption through his blood, even the forgiveness of sins.

Colossians 1:12–14

Therefore watch, and remember, that by the space of three years I ceased not to warn every one night and day with tears.

And now, brethren, I commend you to God, and to the word of his grace, which is able to build you up, and to give you an inheritance among all them which are sanctified.

Acts 20:31–32

Wherein he hath abounded toward us in all wisdom and prudence;

Having made known unto us the mystery of his will, according to his good pleasure which he hath purposed in himself:

That in the dispensation of the fulness of times he might gather together in one all things in Christ, both which are in heaven, and which are on earth; even in him:

In whom also we have obtained an inheritance, being predestinated according to the purpose of him who worketh all things after the counsel of his own will.

Ephesians 1:8–11

O God, when thou wentest forth before thy people, when thou didst march through the wilderness;

The earth shook, the heavens also dropped at the presence of God: even Sinai itself was moved at the presence of God, the God of Israel.

Thou, O God, didst send a plentiful rain, whereby thou didst confirm thine inheritance, when it was weary.

Thy congregation hath dwelt therein: thou, O God, hast prepared of thy goodness for the poor.

The Lord gave the word: great was the company of those that published it.

Psalm 68:7–11

Blessed be the God and Father of our Lord Jesus Christ, which according to his abundant mercy hath begotten us again unto a lively hope by the resurrection of Jesus Christ from the dead,

To an inheritance incorruptible, and undefiled, and that fadeth not away, reserved in heaven for you,

Who are kept by the power of God through faith unto salvation ready to be revealed in the last time.

1 Peter 1:3–5

Our Light

Then spake Jesus again unto them, saying, I am the light of the world: he that followeth me shall not walk in darkness, but shall have the light of life.

John 8:12

In the beginning was the Word, and the Word was with God, and the Word was God.

The same was in the beginning with God.

All things were made by him; and without him was not any thing made that was made.

In him was life; and the life was the light of men.

And the light shineth in darkness; and the darkness comprehended it not.

There was a man sent from God, whose name was John.

The same came for a witness, to bear witness of the Light, that all men through him might believe.

He was not that Light, but was sent to bear witness of that Light.

That was the true Light, which lighteth every man that cometh into the world.

John 1:1–9

The Lord is my light and my salvation; whom shall I fear? The Lord is the strength of my life; of whom shall I be afraid?

When the wicked, even mine enemies and my foes, came upon me to eat up my flesh, they stumbled and fell.

Though an host should encamp against me, my heart shall not fear: though war should rise against me, in this will I be confident.

Psalm 27:1–3

Ye are the light of the world. A city that is set on an hill cannot be hid.

Neither do men light a candle, and put it under a bushel, but on a candlestick; and it giveth light unto all that are in the house.

Let your light so shine before men, that they may see your good works, and glorify your Father which is in heaven.

Matthew 5:14–16

Take heed therefore that the light which is in thee be not darkness.

If thy whole body therefore be full of light, having no part dark, the whole shall be full of light, as when the bright shining of a candle doth give thee light.

Luke 11:35–36

This then is the message which we have heard of him, and declare unto you, that God is light, and in him is no darkness at all.

If we say that we have fellowship with him, and walk in darkness, we lie, and do not the truth:

But if we walk in the light, as he is in the light, we have fellowship one with another, and the blood of Jesus Christ his Son cleanseth us from all sin.

1 John 1:5–7

Then Jesus said unto them, Yet a little while is the light with you. Walk while ye have the light, lest darkness come upon you: for he that walketh in darkness knoweth not whither he goeth.

While ye have light, believe in the light, that ye may be the children of light. . . .

And he that seeth me seeth him that sent me.

I am come a light into the world, that whosoever believeth on me should not abide in darkness.

John 12:35–36, 45–46

Therefore judge nothing before the time, until the Lord come, who both will bring to light the hidden things of darkness, and will make manifest the counsels of the hearts: and then shall every man have praise of God.

1 Corinthians 4:5

Nineteenth-Century Revisions

I n 1870, the Church of England initiated plans for a revision of the King James Version. The reasons given for revision included the outdated English, the progress made by scholars in understanding, and the availability of additional texts of the original biblical languages, especially the Greek text of the New Testament. Two groups of revisers were appointed, one for the Old Testament and one for the New. Before long, parallel companies of revisers were set up in the United States. At first these groups worked under the hope that one version might be produced for both England and the United States. But this was not to be. The American scholars, conservative as they were in their procedure, could not be bound by the stricter conservatism of their British counterparts. The three installments of the British Revised Version (RV) appeared in 1881, in 1885, and in 1894. The American version, or American Standard Version (ASV), was released in 1901, but did not include the Apocrypha.

In 1881, the scholars who developed the Revised Version had this to say about the King James Version:

> We have had to study this great Version carefully and minutely, line by line; and the longer we have been engaged upon it the more we have learned to admire its simplicity, its dignity, its power, its happy turns of expression, its general accuracy, and, we must not fail to add, the music of its cadences and the felicities of its rhythm.

The RV and ASV were solid works of scholarship but did not gain popular acceptance, mainly because their translators, it was said, paid insufficient attention to style and rhythm as they rendered the biblical languages into precise English.

THE

HOLY BIBLE

CONTAINING THE

OLD AND NEW TESTAMENTS

TRANSLATED OUT OF THE ORIGINAL TONGUES

BEING THE VERSION SET FORTH A.D. 1611
COMPARED WITH THE MOST ANCIENT AUTHORITIES AND REVISED
A.D. 1881-1885

Newly Edited by the American Revision Committee
A.D. 1901
STANDARD EDITION

American Bible Society
INSTITUTED IN THE YEAR 1816
PUBLISHED BY
THOMAS NELSON & SONS
NEW YORK

Our Desire

Behold, I was shapen in iniquity; and in sin did my mother conceive me.

Behold, thou desirest truth in the inward parts: and in the hidden part thou shalt make me to know wisdom.

Psalm 51:5–6

Whom have I in heaven but thee? and there is none upon earth that I desire beside thee.

My flesh and my heart faileth: but God is the strength of my heart, and my portion for ever.

Psalm 73:25–26

Thou openest thine hand, and satisfiest the desire of every living thing.

The LORD is righteous in all his ways, and holy in all his works.

The LORD is nigh unto all them that call upon him, to all that call upon him in truth.

Psalm 145:16–18

Delight thyself also in the Lord; and he shall give thee the desires of thine heart.

Psalm 37:4

The fear of the wicked, it shall come upon him: but the desire of the righteous shall be granted.

As the whirlwind passeth, so is the wicked no more: but the righteous is an everlasting foundation.

Proverbs 10:24–25

The desire of the righteous is only good: but the expectation of the wicked is wrath.

Proverbs 11:23

Yea, in the way of thy judgments, O Lord, have we waited for thee; the desire of our soul is to thy name, and to the remembrance of thee.

With my soul have I desired thee in the night; yea, with my spirit within me will I seek thee early: for when thy judgments are in the earth, the inhabitants of the world will learn righteousness.

Isaiah 26:8–9

Brethren, my heart's desire and prayer to God for Israel is, that they might be saved.

Romans 10:1

WHEREFORE LAYING aside all malice, and all guile, and hypocrisies, and envies, and all evil speakings,

As newborn babes, desire the sincere milk of the word, that ye may grow thereby:

If so be ye have tasted that the Lord is gracious.

1 Peter 2:1–3

For this cause we also, since the day we heard it, do not cease to pray for you, and to desire that ye might be filled with the knowledge of his will in all wisdom and spiritual understanding.

Colossians 1:9

The desire of a man is his kindness: and a poor man is better than a liar.

The fear of the Lord tendeth to life: and he that hath it shall abide satisfied; he shall not be visited with evil.

Proverbs 19:22–23

Our Servanthood

And now, Israel, what doth the LORD thy God require of thee, but to fear the LORD thy God, to walk in all his ways, and to love him, and to serve the LORD thy God with all thy heart and with all thy soul.

Deuteronomy 10:12

And if it seem evil unto you to serve the LORD, choose you this day whom ye will serve; whether the gods which your fathers served that were on the other side of the flood, or the gods of the Amorites, in whose land ye dwell: but as for me and my house, we will serve the LORD.

And the people answered and said, God forbid that we should forsake the LORD, to serve other gods;

For the LORD our God, he it is that brought us up and our fathers out of the land of Egypt, from the house of bondage, and which did those great signs in our sight, and preserved us in all the way wherein we went, and among all the people through whom we passed:

And the LORD drave out from before us all the people, even the Amorites which dwelt in the land: therefore will we also serve the LORD; for he is our God.

Joshua 24:15–18

And Samuel said unto the people, Fear not: ye have done all this wickedness: yet turn not aside from following the Lord, but serve the Lord with all your heart; . . .

For the Lord will not forsake his people for his great name's sake: because it hath pleased the Lord to make you his people.

Moreover as for me, God forbid that I should sin against the Lord in ceasing to pray for you: but I will teach you the good and the right way:

Only fear the Lord, and serve him in truth with all your heart: for consider how great things he hath done for you.

1 Samuel 12:20, 22–24

Knowing that of the Lord ye shall receive the reward of the inheritance: for ye serve the Lord Christ.

Colossians 3:24

But Jesus called them unto him, and said, Ye know that the princes of the Gentiles exercise dominion over them, and they that are great exercise authority upon them.

But it shall not be so among you: but whosoever will be great among you, let him be your minister;

And whosoever will be chief among you, let him be your servant:

Even as the Son of man came not to be ministered unto, but to minister, and to give his life a ransom for many.

Matthew 20:25–28

Make a joyful noise unto the L ORD, all ye lands.

Serve the L ORD with gladness: come before his presence with singing.

Know ye that the L ORD he is God: it is he that hath made us, and not we ourselves; we are his people, and the sheep of his pasture.

Enter into his gates with thanksgiving, and into his courts with praise: be thankful unto him, and bless his name.

For the L ORD is good; his mercy is everlasting; and his truth endureth to all generations.

Psalm 100:1–5

How much more shall the blood of Christ, who through the eternal Spirit offered himself without spot to God, purge your conscience from dead works to serve the living God?

Hebrews 9:14

No man can serve two masters: for either he will hate the one, and love the other; or else he will hold to the one, and despise the other. Ye cannot serve God and mammon.

Matthew 6:24

For, brethren, ye have been called unto liberty; only use not liberty for an occasion to the flesh, but by love serve one another.

Galatians 5:13

Our Humility

For thus saith the high and lofty One that inhabiteth eternity, whose name is Holy; I dwell in the high and holy place, with him also that is of a contrite and humble spirit, to revive the spirit of the humble, and to revive the heart of the contrite ones.

Isaiah 57:15

But he giveth more grace. Wherefore he saith, God resisteth the proud, but giveth grace unto the humble.

Submit yourselves therefore to God. Resist the devil, and he will flee from you.

Draw nigh to God, and he will draw nigh to you.

James 4:6–8

Put on therefore, as the elect of God, holy and beloved, bowels of mercies, kindness, humbleness of mind, meekness, longsuffering;

Forbearing one another, and forgiving one another, if any man have a quarrel against any: even as Christ forgave you, so also do ye.

Colossians 3:12–13

By humility and the fear of the LORD are riches, and honour, and life.

Proverbs 22:4

The LORD lifteth up the meek: he casteth the wicked down to the ground.

Sing unto the LORD with thanksgiving; sing praise upon the harp unto our God:

Who covereth the heaven with clouds, who prepareth rain for the earth, who maketh grass to grow upon the mountains.

Psalm 147:6–8

And the servant of the Lord must not strive; but be gentle unto all men, apt to teach, patient, in meekness instructing those that oppose themselves;

If God peradventure will give them repentance to the acknowledging of the truth.

2 Timothy 2:24–25

Likewise, ye younger, submit yourselves unto the elder. Yea, all of you be subject one to another, and be clothed with humility: for God resisteth the proud, and giveth grace to the humble.

Humble yourselves therefore under the mighty hand of God, that he may exalt you in due time:

Casting all your care upon him; for he careth for you.

1 Peter 5:5–7

Our Friend

A friend loveth at all times, and a brother is born for adversity.

Proverbs 17:17

A man that hath friends must shew himself friendly: and there is a friend that sticketh closer than a brother.

Proverbs 18:24

Thine own friend, and thy father's friend, forsake not; neither go into thy brother's house in the day of thy calamity: for better is a neighbour that is near than a brother far off.

Proverbs 27:10

Seest thou how faith wrought with his works, and by works was faith made perfect?

And the scripture was fulfilled which saith, Abraham believed God, and it was imputed unto him for righteousness: and he was called the Friend of God.

James 2:22–23

Greater love hath no man than this, that a man lay down his life for his friends.

Ye are my friends, if ye do whatsoever I command you.

Henceforth I call you not servants; for the servant knoweth not what his lord doeth: but I have called you friends; for all things that I have heard of my Father I have made known unto you.

John 15:13–15

Seest thou how faith wrought with his works, and by works was faith made perfect?

And the scripture was fulfilled which saith, Abraham believed God, and it was imputed unto him for righteousness: and he was called the Friend of God.

James 2:22–23

The poor is hated even of his own neighbour: but the rich hath many friends.

Proverbs 14:20

Our Hope

For thou art my hope, O Lord GOD: thou art my trust from my youth.

By thee have I been holden up from the womb: thou art he that took me out of my mother's bowels: my praise shall be continually of thee.

Psalm 71:5–6

THEREFORE BEING justified by faith, we have peace with God through our Lord Jesus Christ:

By whom also we have access by faith into this grace wherein we stand, and rejoice in hope of the glory of God.

Romans 5:1–2

And hope maketh not ashamed; because the love of God is shed abroad in our hearts by the Holy Ghost which is given unto us.

Romans 5:5

I THEREFORE, the prisoner of the Lord, beseech you that ye walk worthy of the vocation wherewith ye are called,

With all lowliness and meekness, with longsuffering, forbearing one another in love;

Endeavouring to keep the unity of the Spirit in the bond of peace.

There is one body, and one Spirit, even as ye are called in one hope of your calling;

One Lord, one faith, one baptism, one God and Father of all, who is above all, and through all, and in you all.

Ephesians 4:1–6

Wherein God, willing more abundantly to shew unto the heirs of promise the immutability of his counsel, confirmed it by an oath:

That by two immutable things, in which it was impossible for God to lie, we might have a strong consolation, who have fled for refuge to lay hold upon the hope set before us:

Which hope we have as an anchor of the soul, both sure and stedfast, and which entereth into that within the veil;

Whither the forerunner is for us entered, even Jesus, made an high priest for ever after the order of Melchisedec.

Hebrews 6:17–20

For what is our hope, or joy, or crown of rejoicing? Are not even ye in the presence of our Lord Jesus Christ at his coming?

For ye are our glory and joy.

1 Thessalonians 2:19–20

But sanctify the Lord God in your hearts: and be ready always to give an answer to every man that asketh you a reason of the hope that is in you with meekness and fear:

Having a good conscience; that, whereas they speak evil of you, as of evildoers, they may be ashamed that falsely accuse your good conversation in Christ.

For it is better, if the will of God be so, that ye suffer for well doing, than for evil doing.

1 Peter 3:15–17

BEHOLD, WHAT manner of love the Father hath bestowed upon us, that we should be called the sons of God: therefore the world knoweth us not, because it knew him not.

Beloved, now are we the sons of God, and it doth not yet appear what we shall be: but we know that, when he shall appear, we shall be like him; for we shall see him as he is.

And every man that hath this hope in him purifieth himself, even as he is pure.

1 John 3:1–3

Blessed be the God and Father of our Lord Jesus Christ, which according to his abundant mercy hath begotten us again unto a lively hope by the resurrection of Jesus Christ from the dead,

To an inheritance incorruptible, and undefiled, and that fadeth not away, reserved in heaven for you,

Who are kept by the power of God through faith unto salvation ready to be revealed in the last time.

1 Peter 1:3–5

Twentieth- and Twenty-First-Century Revisions

During its long history, the King James Version has been updated and revised several times to reflect changes in speech as well as growing knowledge of the original text of the Scriptures. Previous major revisions of this translation were issued in 1629, 1638, 1762, and 1769.

During the 1970s, Thomas Nelson Publishers, under the direction of president Sam Moore, sensed the need for a fifth major revision of the KJV using updated English and employing the best results of conservative biblical scholarship. Over 130 Bible scholars were selected to work on the New King James Version (NKJV). The translators worked from the earliest and most trustworthy Hebrew and Greek texts available (including the traditional text of the Greek New Testament) and used the 1769 King James revision as its standard to make sure the new edition preserved the majestic style and devotional quality of the original King James.

The most noticeable change in the NKJV is the replacement of "thees" and "thous" and other archaic pronouns with their modern English equivalent. The "est" and "eth" verb endings also were eliminated in favor of more contemporary English forms. The New Testament with Psalms was released in 1980, followed by the full Bible in 1982.

Perfect Trust

And they made war with the Hagarites, with Jetur, and Nephish, and Nodab.

And they were helped against them, and the Hagarites were delivered into their hand, and all that were with them: for they cried to God in the battle, and he was intreated of them; because they put their trust in him.

1 Chronicles 5:19–20

And he said, The Lord is my rock, and my fortress, and my deliverer;

The God of my rock; in him will I trust: he is my shield, and the horn of my salvation, my high tower, and my refuge, my saviour; thou savest me from violence.

2 Samuel 22:2–3

As for God, his way is perfect; the word of the Lord is tried: he is a buckler to all them that trust in him.

For who is God, save the Lord? and who is a rock, save our God?

2 Samuel 22:31–32

But let all those that put their trust in thee rejoice: let them ever shout for joy, because thou defendest them: let them also that love thy name be joyful in thee.

For thou, Lord, wilt bless the righteous; with favour wilt thou compass him as with a shield.

Psalm 5:11–12

The Lord is my rock, and my fortress, and my deliverer; my God, my strength, in whom I will trust; my buckler, and the horn of my salvation, and my high tower.

I will call upon the Lord, who is worthy to be praised: so shall I be saved from mine enemies.

Psalm 18:2–3

Trust in the Lord with all thine heart; and lean not unto thine own understanding.

In all thy ways acknowledge him, and he shall direct thy paths.

Proverbs 3:5–6

Thou wilt keep him in perfect peace, whose mind is stayed on thee: because he trusteth in thee.

Trust ye in the Lord for ever: for in the Lord Jehovah is everlasting strength.

Isaiah 26:3–4

This is a faithful saying and worthy of all acceptation.

For therefore we both labour and suffer reproach, because we trust in the living God, who is the Saviour of all men, specially of those that believe.

These things command and teach.

1 Timothy 4:9-11

In thee, O Lord, do I put my trust: let me never be put to confusion.

Deliver me in thy righteousness, and cause me to escape: incline thine ear unto me, and save me.

Be thou my strong habitation, whereunto I may continually resort: thou hast given commandment to save me; for thou art my rock and my fortress.

Psalm 71:1-3

Trust in the Lord, and do good; so shalt thou dwell in the land, and verily thou shalt be fed.

Delight thyself also in the Lord; and he shall give thee the desires of thine heart.

Commit thy way unto the Lord; trust also in him; and he shall bring it to pass.

And he shall bring forth thy righteousness as the light, and thy judgment as the noonday.

Psalm 37:3-6

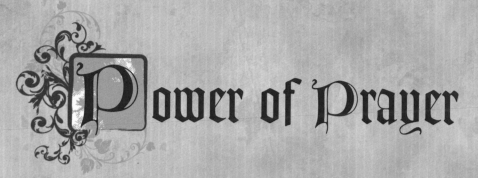

Power of Prayer

If my people, which are called by my name, shall humble themselves, and pray, and seek my face, and turn from their wicked ways; then will I hear from heaven, and will forgive their sin, and will heal their land.

2 Chronicles 7:14

Verily, verily, I say unto you, He that believeth on me, the works that I do shall he do also; and greater works than these shall he do; because I go unto my Father.

And whatsoever ye shall ask in my name, that will I do, that the Father may be glorified in the Son.

If ye shall ask any thing in my name, I will do it.

John 14:12–14

Hear my prayer, O LORD, and let my cry come unto thee.

Hide not thy face from me in the day when I am in trouble; incline thine ear unto me: in the day when I call answer me speedily.

Psalm 102:1–2

Be careful for nothing; but in every thing by prayer and supplication with thanksgiving let your requests be made known unto God.

And the peace of God, which passeth all understanding, shall keep your hearts and minds through Christ Jesus.

Philippians 4:6–7

Call unto me, and I will answer thee, and shew thee great and mighty things, which thou knowest not.

Jeremiah 33:3

Is any sick among you? let him call for the elders of the church; and let them pray over him, anointing him with oil in the name of the Lord:

And the prayer of faith shall save the sick, and the Lord shall raise him up; and if he have committed sins, they shall be forgiven him.

James 5:14–15

Therefore I say unto you, what things soever ye desire, when ye pray, believe that ye receive them, and ye shall have them.

And when ye stand praying, forgive, if ye have ought against any: that your Father also which is in heaven may forgive you your trespasses.

Mark 11:24–25

The LORD is far from the wicked: but he heareth the prayer of the righteous.

Proverbs 15:29

Above all, taking the shield of faith, wherewith ye shall be able to quench all the fiery darts of the wicked.

And take the helmet of salvation, and the sword of the Spirit, which is the word of God:

Praying always with all prayer and supplication in the Spirit, and watching thereunto with all perseverance and supplication for all saints.

Ephesians 6:16–18

earing Fruit

I AM the true vine, and my Father is the husbandman.

Every branch in me that beareth not fruit he taketh away: and every branch that beareth fruit, he purgeth it, that it may bring forth more fruit.

John 15:1–2

I am the vine, ye are the branches: He that abideth in me, and I in him, the same bringeth forth much fruit: for without me ye can do nothing.

If a man abide not in me, he is cast forth as a branch, and is withered; and men gather them, and cast them into the fire, and they are burned.

If ye abide in me, and my words abide in you, ye shall ask what ye will, and it shall be done unto you.

John 15:5–7

And these are they which are sown on good ground; such as hear the word, and receive it, and bring forth fruit, some thirtyfold, some sixty, and some an hundred.

Mark 4:20

For there are three that bear record in heaven, the Father, the Word, and the Holy Ghost: and these three are one.

And there are three that bear witness in earth, the Spirit, and the water, and the blood: and these three agree in one.

1 John 5:7–8

Even so every good tree bringeth forth good fruit; but a corrupt tree bringeth forth evil fruit.

A good tree cannot bring forth evil fruit, neither can a corrupt tree bring forth good fruit.

Every tree that bringeth not forth good fruit is hewn down, and cast into the fire.

Wherefore by their fruits ye shall know them.

Matthew 7:17–20

But the fruit of the Spirit is love, joy, peace, longsuffering, gentleness, goodness, faith,

Meekness, temperance: against such there is no law.

And they that are Christ's have crucified the flesh with the affections and lusts.

If we live in the Spirit, let us also walk in the Spirit.

Let us not be desirous of vain glory, provoking one another, envying one another.

Galatians 5:22–26

Wherefore, my brethren, ye also are become dead to the law by the body of Christ; that ye should be married to another, even to him who is raised from the dead, that we should bring forth fruit unto God.

Romans 7:4

Ye have not chosen me, but I have chosen you, and ordained you, that ye should go and bring forth fruit, and that your fruit should remain: that whatsoever ye shall ask of the Father in my name, he may give it you.

John 15:16

His Delight

Blessed is the man that walketh not in the counsel of the ungodly, nor standeth in the way of sinners, nor sitteth in the seat of the scornful.

But his delight is in the law of the LORD; and in his law doth he meditate day and night.

And he shall be like a tree planted by the rivers of water, that bringeth forth his fruit in his season; his leaf also shall not wither; and whatsoever he doeth shall prosper.

Psalm 1:1–3

If thou turn away thy foot from the sabbath, from doing thy pleasure on my holy day; and call the sabbath a delight, the holy of the LORD, honourable; and shalt honour him, not doing thine own ways, nor finding thine own pleasure, nor speaking thine own words:

Then shalt thou delight thyself in the LORD; and I will cause thee to ride upon the high places of the earth, and feed thee with the heritage of Jacob thy father: for the mouth of the LORD hath spoken it.

Isaiah 58:13–14

Trust in the Lord, and do good; so shalt thou dwell in the land, and verily thou shalt be fed.

Delight thyself also in the Lord; and he shall give thee the desires of thine heart.

Commit thy way unto the Lord; trust also in him; and he shall bring it to pass.

Psalm 37:3–5

Let, I pray thee, thy merciful kindness be for my comfort, according to thy word unto thy servant.

Let thy tender mercies come unto me, that I may live: for thy law is my delight.

Psalm 119:76–77

Wherefore do ye spend money for that which is not bread? and your labour for that which satisfieth not? hearken diligently unto me, and eat ye that which is good, and let your soul delight itself in fatness.

Incline your ear, and come unto me: hear, and your soul shall live; and I will make an everlasting covenant with you, even the sure mercies of David.

Isaiah 55:2–3

But let him that glorieth glory in this, that he understandeth and knoweth me, that I am the Lord which exercise lovingkindness, judgment, and righteousness, in the earth: for in these things I delight, saith the Lord.

Jeremiah 9:24

Who is a God like unto thee, that pardoneth iniquity, and passeth by the transgression of the remnant of his heritage? he retaineth not his anger for ever, because he delighteth in mercy.

Micah 7:18

The LORD possessed me in the beginning of his way, before his works of old.

I was set up from everlasting, from the beginning, or ever the earth was.

When there were no depths, I was brought forth; when there were no fountains abounding with water.

Before the mountains were settled, before the hills was I brought forth:

While as yet he had not made the earth, nor the field, nor the highest part of the dust of the world.

When he prepared the heavens, I was there: when he set a compass upon the face of the depth:

When he established the clouds above: when he strengthened the fountains of the deep:

When he gave to the sea his decree, that the waters should not pass his commandment: when he appointed the foundations of the earth:

Then I was by him, as one brought up with him: and I was daily his delight, rejoicing always before him;

Rejoicing in the habitable part of his earth; and my delights were with the sons of men.

Proverbs 8:22–31

Thou shalt no more be termed Forsaken; neither shall thy land any more be termed Desolate: but thou shalt be called Hephzibah, and thy land Beulah: for the Lord delighteth in thee, and thy land shall be married.

For as a young man marrieth a virgin, so shall thy sons marry thee: and as the bridegroom rejoiceth over the bride, so shall thy God rejoice over thee.

Isaiah 62:4–5

His Sacrifice

Hold thy peace at the presence of the Lord GOD: for the day of the LORD is at hand: for the LORD hath prepared a sacrifice, he hath bid his guests.

And it shall come to pass in the day of the LORD's sacrifice, that I will punish the princes, and the king's children, and all such as are clothed with strange apparel.

Zephaniah 1:7–8

I BESEECH you therefore, brethren, by the mercies of God, that ye present your bodies a living sacrifice, holy, acceptable unto God, which is your reasonable service.

And be not conformed to this world: but be ye transformed by the renewing of your mind, that ye may prove what is that good, and acceptable, and perfect, will of God.

Romans 12:1–2

BE YE therefore followers of God as dear children:

And walk in love, as Christ also hath loved us, and hath given himself for us an offering and a sacrifice to God for a sweetsmelling savour.

Ephesians 5:1–2

For Christ is not entered into the holy places made with hands, which are the figures of the true; but into heaven itself, now to appear in the presence of God for us:

Nor yet that he should offer himself often, as the high priest entereth into the holy place every year with blood of others;

For then must he often have suffered since the foundation of the world: but now once in the end of the world hath he appeared to put away sin by the sacrifice of himself.

Hebrews 9:24–26

Then said he, Lo, I come to do thy will, O God. He taketh away the first, that he may establish the second.

By the which will we are sanctified through the offering of the body of Jesus Christ once for all.

And every priest standeth daily ministering and offering oftentimes the same sacrifices, which can never take away sins:

But this man, after he had offered one sacrifice for sins for ever, sat down on the right hand of God.

Hebrews 10:9–12

Ye also, as lively stones, are built up a spiritual house, an holy priesthood, to offer up spiritual sacrifices, acceptable to God by Jesus Christ.

Wherefore also it is contained in the scripture, Behold, I lay in Sion a chief corner stone, elect, precious: and he that believeth on him shall not be confounded.

1 Peter 2:5–6

By him therefore let us offer the sacrifice of praise to God continually, that is, the fruit of our lips giving thanks to his name.

But to do good and to communicate forget not: for with such sacrifices God is well pleased.

Hebrews 13:15–16

Many scholars praise the King James Bible for its pure English and forceful style, others for its beauty and majesty, and still others for its accurate translation. It is all of that and more. But even more important we must recognize that the King James Version is the Word of God that He has graciously given to His Englishspeaking church. Because its translators strove for accuracy, beauty, power, and literal faithfulness to the Greek and Hebrew texts, the King James Bible has endured as one of the most beloved translations for centuries and today by many is still the translation of choice.